Ken Riley's

Promotional & Novelty Cameras

2025 PRICE GUIDE

Information on HUNDREDS of premium, product, logo, kids, limited editions, generic no-name, giveaways and just plain fun to collect cameras, including price guide, facts and historical data.

Front cover illustration: (1). Charlie the tuna, (2). Donald Duck, (3). Cabbage Patch Kids (4). Muppet Babies (5). Barbie I-Zone (6). Mil-Looney cam (7). Simpsons (8). Iron Man, (9). Kool-Aid (10). Pipo (11.) PokeMon. Cover design: Ken Riley

Acknowledgements:

Much thanks and appreciation to Doug Graham for his help in formatting, editing, and the layout of this book. I also extend my gratitude to both my sons, Eric and Douglas, girlfriend Jae, as well as close friends Tom and Jennifer Lahmers for their help and opinions about my book. I also wish to thank my good friend Jane Buckley for the inspiration that her work with stained glass gave me to create the collage of cameras on the front cover.

TABLE OF CONTENTS

AUTHOR'S STATEMENT

This book represents a lot of time and research to gather enough information about these types of cameras to hopefully be of help to those already collecting and those who may just be starting. First, this book does not have a listing for every camera that is out there. Probably falls rather short but I had to start somewhere. I figure there are hundreds if not thousands of these type cameras to be found and collected, from all over the world. Second, all cameras listed are film cameras and no digital cameras or non-cameras will be listed (such as a squirt camera for instance).

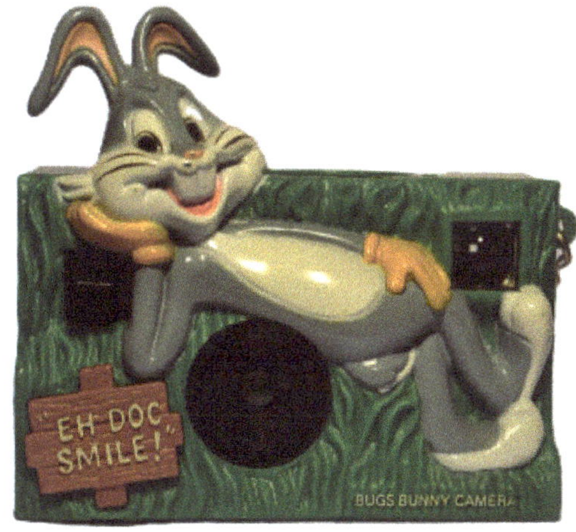

The values stated for each camera represent those that you should typically find a particular camera priced by a seller. Some values will be over-inflated, mainly due to the fact that they will be "moment" driven as in the Barbie cameras and accessories because of the new Barbie movie in theaters as of this writing in 2023. Others will be governed by their scarcity or their over-abundance. My pricing will reflect that. But it's not the end-all to pricing. Remember, this is a guide.

As a collector you will find lots of good buys for many of these cameras. Places to look for deals are yard sales, church rummage sales, local donation shops, and flea markets. You may even have a couple friends or relatives that have some of these cameras they might even give to you. I know I'm wondering how many of these cameras could just be squirreled away in drawers or storage boxes waiting to be rediscovered. Enjoy!

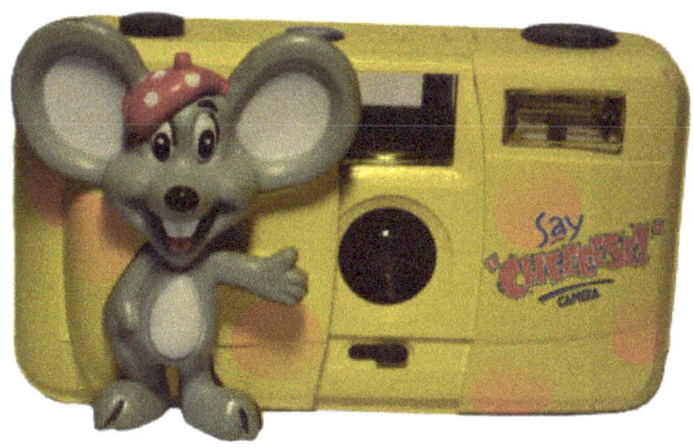

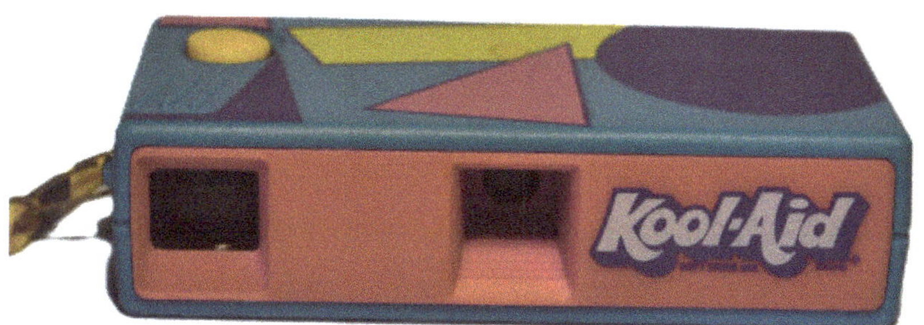

GUIDE to COLLECTING CAMERAS

General Start to Collecting

Collecting as a hobby is a fun and rewarding way of preserving the past and much of its glory as well as personal gratification. I collect cameras. Other people may collect many types of collectible things such as dolls, shot glasses, superheroes, beer steins, plates, you name it, and someone probably collects it. Some folks focus on a particular subject such as Barbie, Pokemon, or Mickey Mouse, for instance, and collect anything and everything about them. Others will collect within a category like I do with cameras.

Seasoned collectors like to acquire, purchase, or trade up to enrich their overall collection value as well as get a new piece. Those of you who are just starting will need to acquire some skills to understand whether the collectible you want to purchase is worth the money. In the case of collecting cameras, I needed to know about the cameras and their values. Looking online I found several books that talked about cameras, lenses, and lots of information about them. And yes, I did purchase them and have been forever grateful that I did.

Now, these books gave me a wealth of information as well as the basic value one should find the for cameras out there. Remember: book values change over time and go out of relevancy at some point. This is understandable when you think about how prices change in our everyday lives.

If the value change is due to a moment-driven force, for instance new Barbie cameras and accessories that were released when the Barbie movie came out in the summer of 2023. Values may be over-inflated because sellers know that they can command higher prices, at least for a while. Most camera values are governed by their scarcity or the over-abundance of them.

Lets Talk Condition

I'm going to talk mainly about cameras from here on as that's what I collect and mostly know about. Ok, you found an antique or novelty camera you would like to own. The first thing you want to do is determine whether it's in good condition or not.

You'll need to judge the camera for its looks:

Does it look like a nice piece?

Are there things wrong such as any scratches, nicks, broken parts, or missing parts?

Is it dirty and/or rusty or cracked?

Is the lens clear or foggy?

Is there a take-up spool?

(Most old roll-film cameras should have one, although they are rather easy to obtain.)

Next, you will want to find out if it functions or not. Check to see if the shutter operates and if there are f/stop apertures, are they functioning? Does the camera have folding bellows? Then make sure they operate correctly and fairly smoothly. Is the camera a box type? Click the shutter and look through the viewfinder. Examine the outside of the camera for signs of rust, wear level of edges, and if it has a camera carry strap- is it in good condition, bad, or non-existent?

If all you plan to do is display it and don't care if it works or not then you'll want to move to the next step which is whether it comes with any other things such as an original box, camera case, flash cubes, bulbs, or units, additional lenses, film, lens filters, original pamphlets, and so on. Having extras to go with a camera can either make or break a deal in some cases.

In the case that you are buying from a seller at a yard sale, flea market, or church bazaar, you'll find that many, if not most, of the sellers don't actually know the value of all the things they sell. If they have an antique camera, they may not know its value and either price it way over or much lower than a book price may indicate. Either way,] you'll want to barter some for the item. I mean, after all, it's a yard sale; and they are doing it to unload the stuff they don't want.

Functionality

If you want the piece to be fully functional then you'll need to check whether the shutter operates correctly or not. Operating some models can be as easy as clicking the shutter control back and forth. Many box cameras operate this way. However, you may be checking out a model that has shutter speed settings. Here, you may need to select a speed and "cock" the shutter to be used when you are ready to take the picture. Be sure to check all the speeds if they have multiple shutter speeds. Old cameras have a way of sticking due to age and the lubrication level (or lack there of) of the shutter mechanisms.

While you're checking the shutter don't forget to check the apertures of the lens to make sure they operate smoothly and as they should. Set the lens at f/22 and see if it is f/22. Set the f stops throughout the aperture range of the camera and click the shutter to be sure the f stops are where they should be.

While you are operating the shutter and lens apertures, check the clarity of the lens. Old camera lenses will sometimes cloud up due to moisture getting into the lens assembly because of the cracking of the seals around the lens housing. If you are enterprising enough you can disassemble the lens unit and clean the lens. There are books on the market that explain things like this.

Next, you'll want to look through the viewfinder to see if it's clear and in good condition. There are many different types of viewfinder configurations you may encounter. These include optical, folding type, wire type, waist level, and ground glass.

An example of an optical finder is usually found on a 35mm camera where you look through the finder and see the picture framing. A folding type finder is usually found on bellows-type cameras and some of the cheap plastic novelty ones. The wire types are mostly found on the old box cameras and they just pull out to form a framing for your picture.

What is called a waist-level viewfinder is one usually found on the old box cameras—one for the vertical shot, one for the horizontal shot. The ground glass type is usually found on larger cameras such as view cameras that take pictures on film formats like 4x5, and 8x10 for example.

If the camera has a metering system; what are the battery requirements? Same question if the camera has other functions that require power. If you plan to use the camera to take shots you'll want to know if the system works. Some cameras require a battery to power the shutter and/ or film advance. Is the battery still available? Once again, though, it depends on whether you intend to use the camera or simply display it.

Film

Some older cameras can still be used because the films are still being made, although not necessarily in the United States. Most of these films are made overseas in Europe, Germany, Japan, and elsewhere.

Finding and purchasing the old roll films is one thing; now you have to find a processing lab to develop the film. The internet is a wonderful place to find resources and I recommend you search there for a lab.

Some film will not be available no matter how much you search. The 126 film cartridge for instance is only available unless it's old, outdated stock. This film is no longer produced by anyone. The 110 cartridge films are available through private film labs and dealers and you will have to do some searching on the internet to find this film. These dealers will reload empty 110 cartridges with 16mm motion picture film. The cameras that this size film fits don't rely on sprocket holes to drive the film as you advance from frame to frame taking pictures.

However, the 35mm roll films are still made by a variety of manufacturers. Many, if not most, of the novelty plastic cameras made in the last 20-25 years use 35mm film and the processing of this film is much easier to come by. Many stores and pharmacies offer 35mm color film processing. In the back section of this book find a listing of places, links, and information about films and film processing.

Repairs and Problems

Let's understand that there is nothing "mint" about an old camera. It may appear as a super nice example of a certain model camera but there may be underlying things that could impact the value of the piece. On the other hand, there are many fine examples of old and antique cameras that won't need any attention other than you placing it on your shelf. But understand that cameras that are 50, 60, 80, or even a 100 years old may have problems.

For example: I found a novelty camera on eBay that I'd love to add to my collection. Once I received it, though, I found that the shutter/aperture didn't operate correctly. To repair I'll have to try to take the camera apart and see what the problem is. Had I been able to see and hold the camera I would have found the problem and then been able to say yes or no to the transaction based on that assessment. By the same token, I've purchased several cameras from online sellers that were just fine and how described.

Many old cameras can be repaired simply by acquiring another camera of the same model that is also broken in another way, and using the good parts of it to fix up yours. Other issues may be that the camera needs a good cleaning and maybe some lubrication or a spring needs reset to operate the shutter. The lens of old cameras tend to fog over time and requires that the lens assembly be taken apart and cleaned—no easy task for some cameras.

Another issue is with the cameras that have bellows. Some cameras had the colored bellows that they came with replaced with black ones because the original one had prematurely deteriorated. This was usually due to the caustic nature of the dyes used in coloring the bellows. They would crack and/or develop light-leak holes and render the camera rather useless.

One of the more famous cameras that had this problem is the Kodak Boy Scout folding camera of 1929-1933 that originally came with a green colored bellows. Many were replaced with a black one so you may find examples with either the green or black bellows. The cameras that still have the original colored bellows are worth more than the ones with a replacement black bellows; usually much more.

Pricing of Cameras

I mentioned earlier that I had purchased books about cameras and their pricing. The one source that is invaluable to me or any other camera collector is a pricing book that was put out by James M. McKeown. He authored his camera pricing books for over 40 years; McKeown's Price Guide to Antique and Classic Cameras. Any of his books going back 25 years would be good ones to own. Truly, any serious camera collector or dealer would want this book in their arsenal.

Another book I'll recommend is one put out by Michael McBroom in 2000, the 6th edition. It too is an older book but has just tons of information about cameras, their lenses, and accessories. So, between these two books and the internet, you should be able to learn about and find the cameras of your dreams. Now remember the information contained in these books is what is of great importance; not so much the pricing which after enough time goes by may/will be irrelevant.

In Closing

One thing that needs to be understood about cameras is that they don't change value that quickly. However, the values have changed for some models while others are still flat. Once again it goes back to how many of the cameras are still out there and available. Kodak made millions of camera models so there are still many thousands of them left which keeps the value from moving up much. But some camera makers only made a few of their cameras and went out of business or sold out to a bigger name.

Some of these cameras are worth hundreds and even many thousands of dollars.

Hence why I recommend the two books I referenced above. The information is worth the weight in gold. I don't receive any type of compensation for recommending these books. They are just the best books for the serious collector.

A quick search on eBay, Google, Yahoo!, Bing, or any search sirte reveals what sellers are asking for any particular camera model. Always remember that there are many sites and sellers on the internet to find the camera or equipment you are looking for.

Films and Film Processing

List of currently available photographic films (all types, all years): https://en.wikipedia.org/wiki/List_of_photographic_films

Online guide to "Where to Develop Film in 2024" (by PetaPixel): https://petapixel.com/where-to-develop-film/

Film Processing Links:

Graination: Film developing and printing; negative and positive (E-6) films; Toronto, ON, Canada - https://graination.ca/

All Things Film: Disposable camera, 35mm, 120 roll films, E-6, photo printing. North London, ON, Canada - https://www.allthingsfilm.ca/

The Darkroom: Film developing and printing; San Clemente, CA, USA - https://thedarkroom.com/

Reformed Film Lab: Film developing and printing; 35mm & 120 roll films; color or B/W. Ormond Beach, FL, USA - https://reformedfilmlab.com/

Other local USA locations: 35mm film, processing, printing, other.

CVS

Walmart

Walgreens

Motion picture links

Cine Lab: Motion picture services; 8mm, 16mm, 35mm negative and positive processing; film scanning; more; New Bedford, MA, USA - https://www.cinelab.com/

Supaphoto Ltd.: Cine films transfers; 8mm, super 8, 9.5mm and 16mm; Brighton, East Sussex, UK - https://supaphoto.com/

Spectra Film & Video: Cine film processing, scanning, films, more; North Hollywood, CA, USA - https://spectrafilmandvideo.com/

THE CAMERAS

Accident Documentation Camera Kit (2007)

This disposable camera is part of a kit designed to help you document an automobile accident. The kit includes a flash camera preloaded with 35mm film, a step-by-step guide, fact form, witness cards, pencil, and reminder decal. The camera itself has a cheap plastic body with a yellow cardboard covering that states "Accident Camera" on the face as well as printed "Caution Strips" across the top and bottom. Copyrighted 2007 by AxiKit, Inc., and distributed by the Galaxy Group.

$2-$12, camera alone; $15-$25, in original packaging

Aladdin 35mm Fun Saver Camera (1993)

This outdoor single-use camera was made and packaged by Kodak for The Walt Disney Company as a promotion for Disney's Aladdin animated movie which came out near the end of 1992. In addition, the film was a box office sensation and the highest earning film of 1992-93 grossing over $504 million world wide.

The camera comes preloaded with Kodak Gold Ultra 27 exposure, ISO 400, 35mm color print film. It has a fixed focus-free lens and simple mechanical shutter; no flash. The first picture on the roll of film is a photo of Aladdin along with Princess Jasmine floating on the magic carpet and the wish granting genie emerging from his lamp. Original price was around $7.50. It was made in the USA by Eastman Kodak Company. ©Walt Disney Productions, Inc.

$5-$15 for camera alone; $20-$30 in unopened original box/package

More about the movie Aladdin here: https://en.wikipedia.org/wiki/Aladdin_(1992_Disney_film)

Aladdin Fun Mini Camera (1992)

This is a plastic bodied camera with a cardboard covering depicting a photo of Aladdin with Princess Jasmine afloat on the magic carpet along with the Kodak and Disney logos. The camera was a promotion for the Disney animated film "Aladdin" which premiered near the end of 1992. Additionally, the film was a box office sensation and the highest earning film of 1992-93 grossing over $504 million world wide. This is a single use camera and comes preloaded with 27 exposure, ISO 400, Kodak Gold Ultra 35mm color print film; no flash. It was made in the USA by Eastman Kodak Company. ©Walt Disney Productions, Inc. and is uncommon.

$5-$15 for camera alone; $20-$30 in unopened original box/package

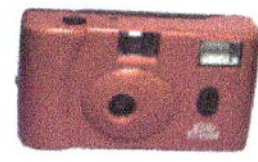

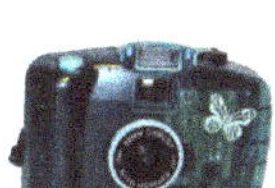

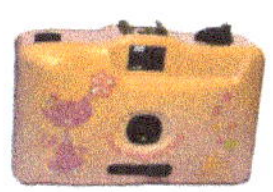

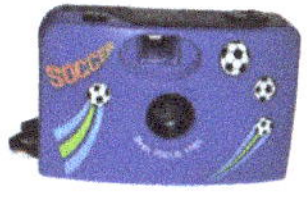

AGH 35mm Camera (1990s)

An all-black plastic camera with the letters "AGH" and words "Allegheny General Hospital"[1] printed on the face below the flash. It was likely a hand-out to staff and/or patients as a promotion for the hospital. This is a basic point-and-shoot 35mm reusable camera with an electronic flash and a carry strap. It was made for Kinetic of New York, NY, USA, in China.

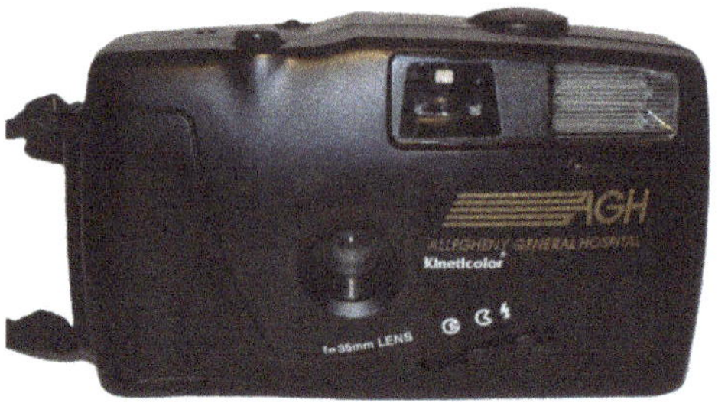

$5-$15

Allegheny General Hospital, a part of the Allegheny Health Network

(https://www.ahn.org) in Pittsburgh, PA, USA, has roots going back to 1881.

A complete history is available here: https://bit.ly/Allegheny_Gene

Alligator 35mm "Creature Cameras" Camera (1986)

This camera is from the "Creature Camera" series by Kids Can Press* and licensed by Provincial Products, Inc. It was part of their promotion of "Franklin the Turtle" book series and books about "Elliot Moose".

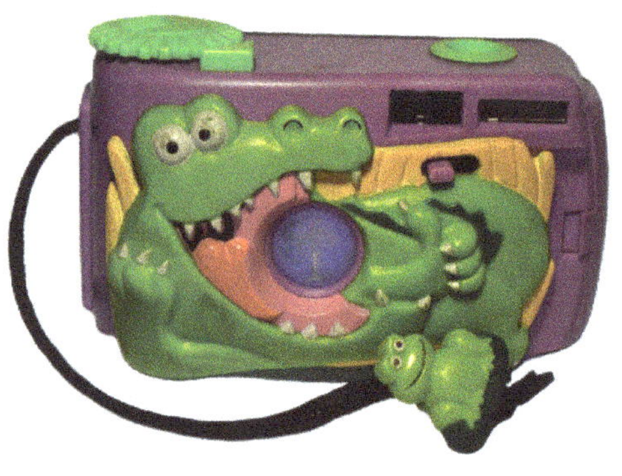

There is a large relief image of an alligator on front of camera and a frog on the carry strap. Simple one click shutter and focus free lens and uses 35mm roll films. Flash models require two AAA batteries. Other "Creature Camera" series cameras include Franklin the Turtle, Batman & Robin, Polar Bear, Monkey, Cat & Mouse, Crocodile, Caterpillar, Sesame Street, Rugrats, and famous Looney Tunes characters. It is manufactured in China by Vivitar Corporation; ©Provincial Products, Inc.; Uncommon.

$20-$50

*Kids Can Press, Toronto, Ontario is a children's book publishing company.

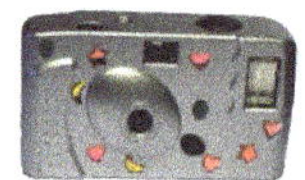

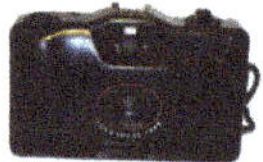

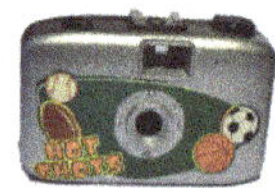

American Girl I-Zone Camera by Polaroid (2000)

This Polaroid version of an American Girl camera produces small (36mm x 24mm) images on Polaroid "Pocket Film". Camera was sold as a complete kit and included a 6 exposure film pack and two type 'AA' batteries to power the built-in electronic flash (unlike other Polaroid integral films, this new Pocket Film does not contain its own power source). In addition to standard prints, a special film is available to allow the camera to produce small photographic stickers as well. Simple one click shutter and focus free lens.

The I-Zone camera was introduced in 1999 and was originally available in a choice of three bright colors- vibrant green, red, and blue. Some special variants have also since appeared, such as a Barbie®-themed camera (with matching accessories), and a "Millennium Silver" edition. Besides American Girl, there is Tweety Bird, Hello Kitty, among others also to be found. Many other colors were introduced over the years such as purple and pastel colors and even translucent versions. American Girl is a trademark of the Pleasant Company, Middleton, Wisconsin and now owned by Mattel Corp. It was manufactured in Japan by Polaroid Corporation.

$5-$15

https://en.wikipedia.org/wiki/American_Girl

Argus Mini Palmatic 110 Camera (1977)

A small palm-size mini-camera made by Argus[1] for type 110 cartridge films. It sports a mechanical shutter with a speed of 1/90th of a second and a 25mm, f/9.5 fixed-focus Cintar lens. It uses either a flip-flash (8-pack) or an available electronic flash via a hot shoe. It is available in gold, silver, or black. The Mini Palmatic 2 comes with a built-in electronic flash and was made in British Hong Kong.

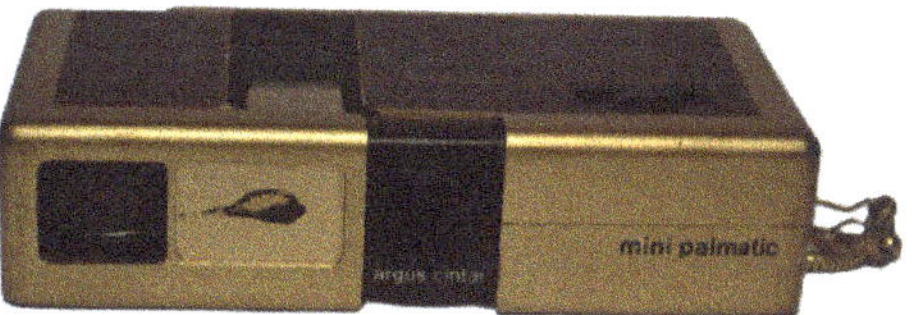

$5-$15, camera alone; $20-$40, in original packaging

Argus produced many camera models over the years including movie cameras, movie projectors, and 35mm slide projectors. Argus was also a leading supplier of military cameras, binoculars, periscopes, and gun sights during World War II and the Korean War. Today, Argus products include a wide variety of digital imaging cameras and video products. They are now located near Chicago, in Elk Grove Village, IL, USA.

Babette Camera (1960s)

A plastic camera offered as a chewing gum premium by the bubblegum giant Bazooka. The body of the camera is a hard plastic and comes in various colors. It uses type 127 roll-film and takes 16 pictures per roll and has a simple one-click shutter. It was made in Hong Kong.

$1-$10

Bacon Disposable Flash Camera (2003)

A cheap plastic camera with a cardboard cover with images of bacon and a flying pig with the word "Bacon" printed across the top of the face. It has an electronic flash and comes preloaded with 24-exposure, 35mm color-print film. Every photo contains one of six phrases and images about bacon that show up when you get the film processed and printed. In addition, there are six surprise graphics for your enjoyment. It was likely used as a promotional giveaway to increase bacon sales. It was made in China.

$5-$15

Bananas in Pyjamas Camera (1995)

This plastic yellow colored (face) reusable camera features the two Bananas in Pyjamas television show characters; mischievous twins B1 and B2 on the face. The Children's TV series ran from 1992 until 2001 and aired on the ABC TV network in Australia.

It has a 35mm fixed-focus optical lens and simple one-click shutter; no flash and nowhere to mount one; uses standard 35mm roll-films; optical viewfinder and carry strap. This was a giveaway to promote the Bananas in Pyjamas children's TV show. When shown in the USA, the title was revised to read "Bananas in Pajamas" dropping the "y" to make it more American. ©Australian Broadcasting Corp.; made in China.

$1-$10

More information about the show can found here: https://bit.ly/Bananas_in_Pyjamas

the Barbie section

Barbie 35mm Camera with Flash (2008)

This Barbie camera is done in colors of pink and white with a large oval area around lens that is a darker pink with a flower design within. It is reusable and seems to be of reasonable construction to last a long time. The camera ensemble included one roll of 10 exposures; ISO 200: "Barbie" 35mm color print film and one type AA battery to power the flash; has optical viewfinder and preset fixed focus lens; one click shutter. The ensemble was made in China and distributed by KIDdesigns, Inc., Rahway, NJ, USA; ©Mattel, Inc.

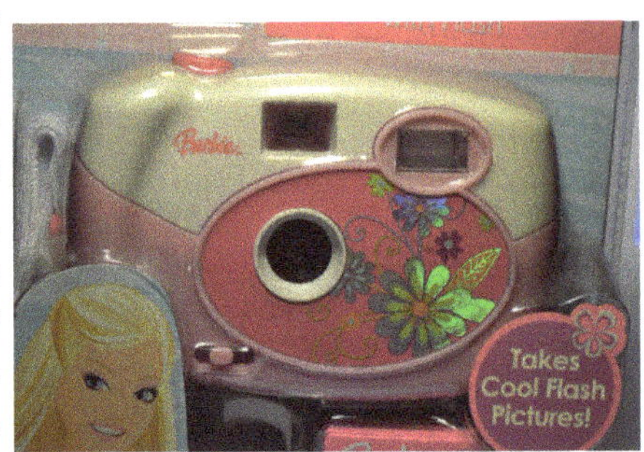

$90-$200 in original packaging, $20-$50 camera alone

Barbie Three Piece Photo Fun Set (1995)

A trim-line style pink plastic camera with a heart shape design around the lens as well as a picture of Barbie in a heart shape on face. The complete set included a camera, photo album, and a Barbie 110 film cartridge (12-exposure, ISO 200). It is a simple one-click operation with no flash and is fairly common.

$5-$10, camera only; $15-$30, for the complete original set

Barbie Cameramatic (1978)

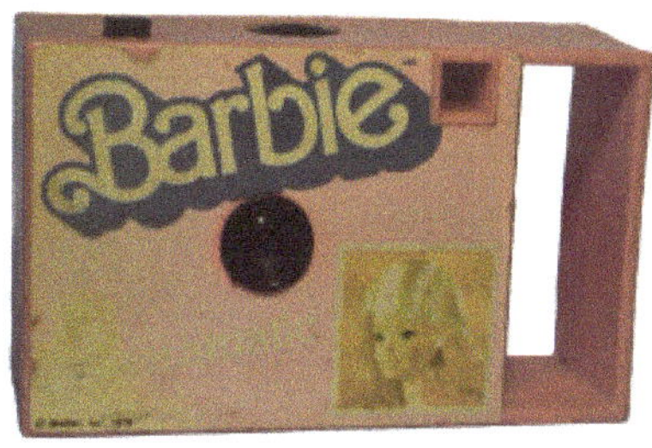

The original camera that started the Barbie cameras series, it was introduced in 1978 for the price of $9.99. The camera is made of pink plastic and has a built-in viewfinder, a f/5.6 glass lens, used type 126 cartridge films and flash-cubes for indoor photos. Made in Hong Kong for Mattel, Inc., and licensed by Vanity Fair, Inc.

$20-$40

Similar Barbie Cameras:

These camera sets all have the same Barbie trim-line style camera but vary in what each set comes with. Some had the camera and film cartridge; another had the camera, a photo album, and a film cartridge; while yet another offered the camera and a miniature toy camera as an accessory for the Barbie doll. These cameras began in the early 1990s and were sold through the decade. They are common and are made in China.

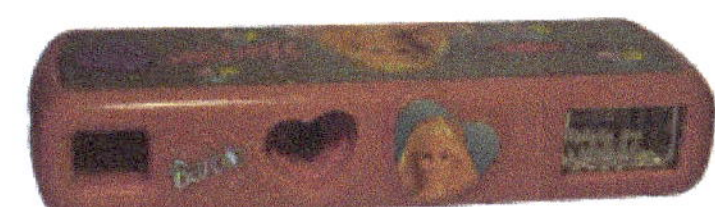

- Barbie Glitter Star Outdoor 110 Camera (including the rectangle ones without the heart shape around the lens)
- Barbie Photo Fun Sets (all)
- Barbie 110 Camera Set (1996), (1998)
- Barbie Hollywood Star Outfit (1995)
- Barbie 5 Piece Flash Photo Fun Set (1995)
- Barbie 4 Piece Photo Fun Set (1997)
- Barbie "Jelly" Cameras (all)

$15-$25, camera alone; $20-$45, in original packaging

Barbie Disposable Camera (2002)

A generic single-use camera with a plastic body and a cardboard covering that depicts a pink swirl design with a picture of Barbie on the front and has Malibu Barbie printed on the bottom front of the camera. This camera was part of a hand-out souvenir from the 2002 National Barbie Doll Collectors Convention held in Denver, CO, USA. It comes preloaded with a 12-exposure roll of 35mm color print film, has a built-in electronic flash, simple one-click shutter, and a plastic fixed-focus lens. It was made in China.

$5-$15

Barbie Fun Fashion 35mm Camera with Flash (1999)

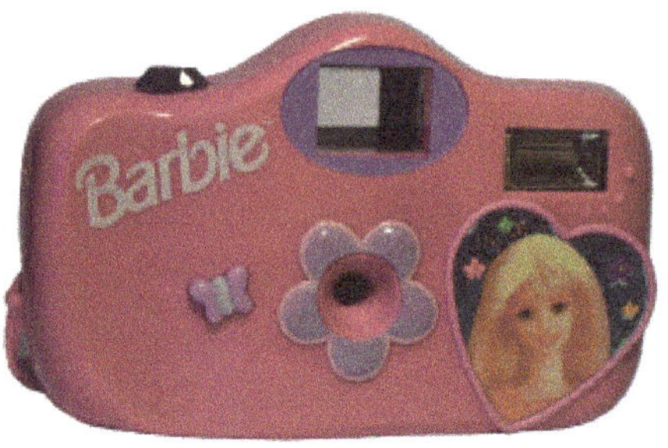

This is a pink plastic camera with a picture of Barbie on the face. There are flowers also present with the larger of them around the lens. The camera uses 35mm film and comes with a miniature toy camera as an accessory for a Barbie doll. These cameras come in a variety of colors, some without a flash as well, and are commonly found. It was made in China by the Tiffen Co., LLC, and copyrighted by Mattel, Inc.

$5-$10

Barbie Glitter Star Camera (1994)

A pink plastic camera with a lens set in a heart shape. Barbie is also on the face, set in a heart shape as well. The camera has a miniature non-functioning toy version of the real camera as

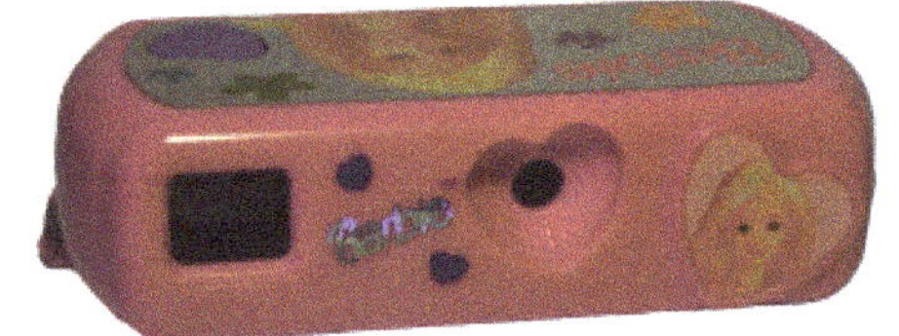

an accessory for a Barbie doll and a set of binoculars. The camera is reusable and uses type 110 cartridge films. It has a simple one-speed shutter, fixed-focus lens, and no flash. Copyrighted by Mattel, Inc., and made in China.

$5-$15, camera only; $15-$35, in original packaging

Barbie Polaroid 600 Instant Camera (1999)

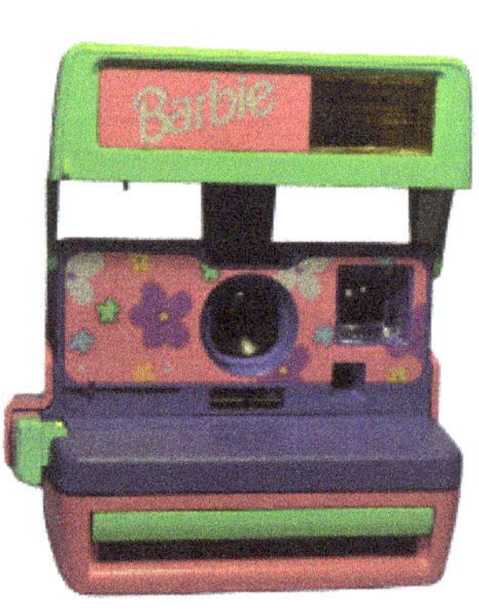

An instant Barbie camera made by Polaroid. It has the Barbie colors of pink, green, and purple. Another version with colors of yellow and pink is also available called "Malibu Barbie." These Polaroid cameras use type 600 instant film and have a 110mm, f/10 fixed lens. The exposures are automatic with speeds of 1/3 to 125th of a second and the camera has a manual slider control to lighten/darken the photo. A flash is built-in and has a manual override. Battery power was built into the film pack, common in Polaroid cameras.

$169 Refurbished

Barbie I-Zone Camera by Polaroid (1999)

Introduced in 1999, this camera used a special Polaroid instant "Pocket Film." Although the picture size is the same as that of 35mm film (24 x 36mm), they do not use standard 35mm roll-films. The films for the I-zone models were discontinued in 2006. This and other "Special Markets I-Zone" models were actually manufactured for Polaroid by Tomy, a Japanese toy maker.

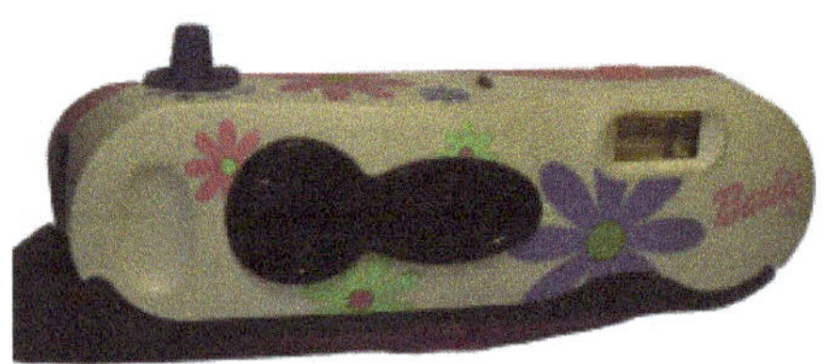

Other features are a focus-free lens, a built-in selectable flash, and a manual film advance. The power source is two AA batteries, unlike so many of the Polaroid cameras that had the power source built into the film pack.

$50-$150

Barbie White (Hanimex) 35mm Camera (2002)

An almost all-white plastic camera that has Barbie printed on the front along with Hanimex,[1] the name of the camera supplier. The front of the camera is white, while the control knobs and the backdoor of the film compartment is black. The camera uses 35mm roll-films and has a hot-shoe for a flash. It was made in China.

$5-$15; more if in original packaging

Fuji Film Company acquired Hanimex from NRG Overseas Investment Ltd. of Ricoh Company, Ltd. in 2004. The Hanimex name was then discontinued. In its day, Hanimex sold cameras, lenses, and projectors.

Much more information about the company can be found here: https://bit.ly/Hanimex-Wiki

Batgirl 35mm Camera (1997)

This is a single-use, cheap plastic camera with a wrap-around cardboard cover depicting Batgirl on the face. It came preloaded with 24-exposure, ISO 400, 35mm film with no flash. It was made in China.

$5-$15, camera alone; $15-$30, in good condition and in original packaging

Other cameras to look for include Batman, Robin, Mr. Freeze, and Dynamic Duo, all disposable types.

Batman 35mm Camera (2005)

This 35mm Batman camera has a shadowed "Batman" picture on the front. The outfit comes with a camera, an electronic flash, 12-exposure roll of "Batman film," a AAA battery, wrist strap with a simple one-click shutter and focus-free lens. This was part of merchandise sold after the movie "Batman Begins" was released. Licensed by Provincial Products, Inc., Ontario, Canada, it was made in China.

$5-$10, camera only; $10-$25, for complete outfit

Batman Adventure Kit with Camera (2010-2019)

This camera and kit is a promo for a 2012 Batman movie "The Dark Knight Rises," a sequel film to the 2008 "The Dark Knight." The kit contains a camera, flashlight, and binoculars. The reusable camera uses 35mm roll-films, but has no flash, and has a rather cheap pop-up view-finder. It was made in China.

$5-$15, camera alone; $20-$35 in original packaging

Batman Spy Adventure Kit with Camera (1997)

This adventure kit comes with a 35mm camera (no flash), binoculars, compass, telescope, and flashlight. It was made in China.

$5-$15, camera alone; $20-$35 in original packaging

Batman and Robin 35mm Flash Camera (1997)

A hard plastic 35mm camera depicting Batman and Robin. It features a flash and focus-free plastic lens. ISO 400 film was recommended but not included with the camera. It also came with a one year guarantee. It was distributed by Provincial Products Inc., Mississauga, ON, Canada, and made in China.

$10-$20

Best Western Super-Hero Cameras (1997)

These cameras were a promo gift from Best Western Hospitality Group as part of their "Summer Adventure" vacation promotion when you stayed with them at one of their properties. Cameras are disposable, with a simple shutter and lens, no flash, and comes preloaded with 24-exposure Fujicolor Superia X-TRA 35mm film. Copyrights belonged to Best Western Hospitality Group., Fuji Photo Corp, Inc. and D.C. Comics. They were made in China.

$10-$20

- Superfriends: Superman, Wonder Woman, Batman, and The Flash
- Superman
- Batman, Wonder Woman, Superman
- Batman

Betty Boop Simple-Use 35mm Camera (2023)

This reusable camera features an all red face with Betty Boop and her dog clearly displayed and her name spelled out in yellow. The camera is sold preloaded with 27-exposure, 35mm, ISO 400 roll-film. It also includes an AA battery to power a built-in electronic flash. The lens is a 31mm, f/11 fixed-focus type with a 1/125th second shutter speed. It was made in China.

$29

This camera is in current production and available here: https://bit.ly/BettyBoopCamera

Big Lots! Camera (1999)

This is a plastic point and shoot 35mm camera given as part of a promotion when you joined Big Lots! "Buzz Club" and has "Big Lots!" printed on the front of the camera. It uses 35mm roll-films and is reusable, but with no flash or hot shoe. It was made in China.

$1-$10

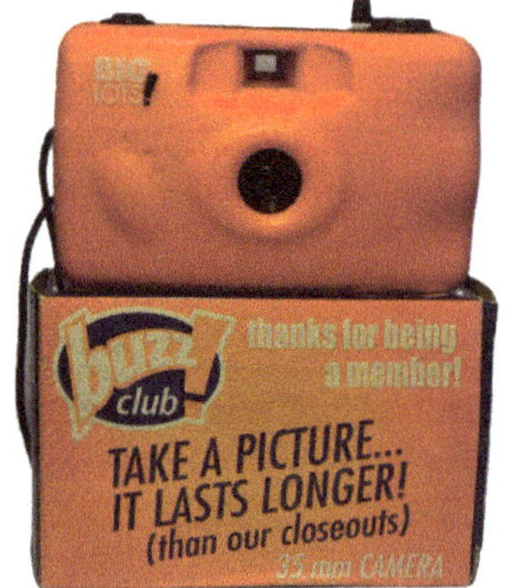

Bilora Bellina 127 Camera (1963)

The Bellina model is a compact camera with a rectangular collapsible front and uses type 127 roll-films. The lens is a Biloxar f/5.6 with distance scale and there are four settings for the shutter; B, 30, 60, 125. The camera has a rapid-wind lever similar to 35mm cameras and came in a fitted case with flash-gun and instructions. This model also is known by two other names which are "Motorist's Outfit" or "Auto Belina".

Bilora brand cameras were first produced starting in 1935 in a factory located in Radevormwald, Germany. The Bellina model was introduced in 1963 and, according to McKeown's Camera Price Guide were still being sold in 1980 for about $18.00. This being somewhat unusual because the factory had ceased camera making operations in 1975. Most agree however that the Bilora line of cameras were of high quality for their modest price.

$40-$75

The brand name BILORA has been created using the names of the company's founder - Wilhelm Kür-BI, Carl NiggeLOh - and the city of the company headquarters RAdevormwald.

Blue Man Group Camera (2008)

A plastic disposable camera with cardboard wrap-around depicting one of the Blue Man Group members, his eyes staring at you. It comes preloaded with 27-exposure, ISO 400, 35mm color print film and a battery to power the flash. It is uncommon. Printed, packaged, and assembled in the United States.

$15-$30

Bomb Pop Camera (2000s)

A plastic point and shoot camera with a printed wrap-around cardboard covering depicting the words "Bomb Pop[1] Summer" and others all over front and back. It came preloaded with a roll of 35mm film and battery for the electronic flash. It is a promotion for the frozen Bomb Pop confections. It was made in China.

$1-$10

Bomb Pop frozen pops were invented and founded in Kansas City, MO, USA, in 1955. In 1991, Wells Dairy, now Wells Enterprises, purchased the Bomb Pop business. As of 2015, the company offered nine main Bomb Pop flavors plus others.
More found here: bit.ly/bomb_pop

BomberMan 35mm Camera (1996)

A plastic camera with the Japanese animated video game character BomberMan[1] on its face. This camera is reusable and came with a roll of 12-exposure, ISO 100, 35mm roll-film. There is built-in flash and has a hot shoe for an external flash. It has a focus-free 35mm, f/8 lens. It was copyrighted 1996 by Hudson Soft and made in China.

$50-$100

The Bomber Man video game was developed by Hudson Soft and released in Japan in 1983. The game series had sold over 10 million copies by 1998. Super Bomber Man R2 was released in late 2023. The Bomber Man franchise is currently owned by Konami.
https://bit.ly/hudson_bomberman

Book 110 Camera (1970s)

This one is in the shape of a [small] book and came in a couple different title names like Donkey or Webster's Dictionary. There was a book case that the "book camera" would slide into to store and hide. The camera has a fixed-focus 23mm, f/8 lens; 1/80th sec. shutter speed; optical viewfinder; and used 110 cartridge films; no flash. It can be found in various colors and was made in Japan.

$40-$60 camera alone; $80-$100 with original case.

Bratz Birthday Camera (2007)

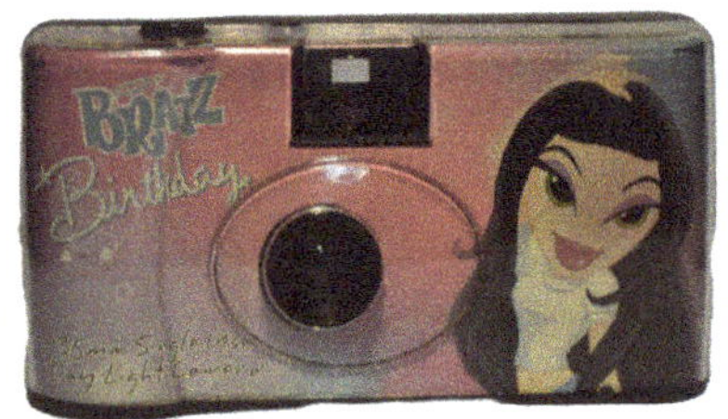

This is a single-use camera and a Bratz doll together as a set. The camera came preloaded with a roll of 35mm, 12-exposure color print film. It has no flash and a focus-free lens. It was copyrighted by MGA Entertainment, Inc., and made in China.

$5-$15, camera only; $50-$100 in original packaging

Bratz "The Movie" Camera (2007)

A plastic 35mm camera that resembles a real 35mm camera and flash. The camera was a promotion for the movie Bratz. It has a sticker that states "Bratz The Movie" on the back of the body. It has a simple lens and shutter. It is copyrighted by MGA Entertainment, Inc., and made in China.

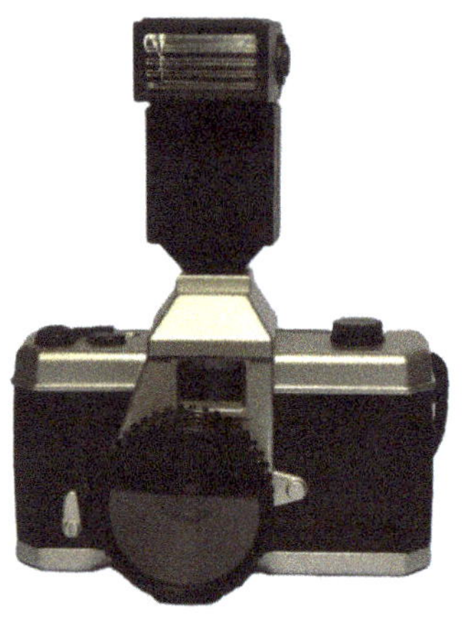
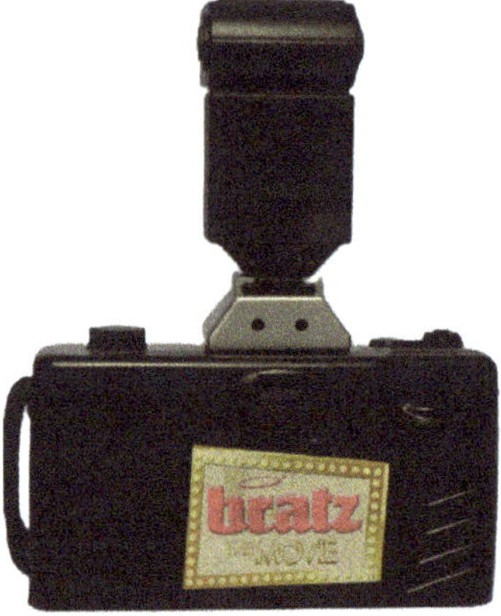
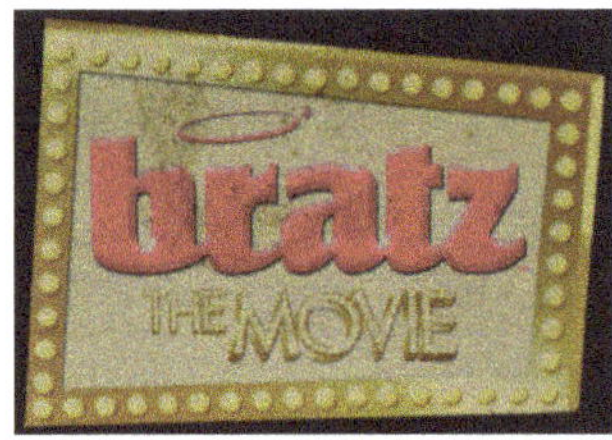

$10-$20, camera only; $70-$110 (if in original packaging with a Bratz doll or other Bratz accessories/kits)

Bratz The Movie was released in 2007 based on a doll toy line and produced by MGA Entertainment. Unfortunately, the film didn't do well and was a commercial failure after spending $20M to produce the film and only grossing around $26M worldwide. More here: https://bit.ly/BratzFilm

Bratz Rock Angelz Disposable Camera (2005)

This is a camera with a cheap body that has a cardboard covering with "Rock Angelz" printed all over the face. It comes preloaded with 27-exposure, 35mm film rated at ISO 400. It has a focus-free lens, single-speed shutter, built-in electronic flash powered by an included single AA battery. It was trademarked and copyrighted by MGA Entertainment, Inc., and made in China.

$15-$30

Bugs Bunny 110 Photo Outfit (1998)

This outfit consists of a cartridge of 110 Looney Tunes color print film, photo album and stickers, and a reusable 110 plastic camera with Bugs Bunny's image on the front. It had a simple shutter and fixed focus lens. Other outfit versions contained binoculars with Bugs Bunny's face on top. This camera originally came in either a cardboard box or blister packaging. Values for both are given below.

$10-$20, camera alone; $30-$50, complete in original blister packaging; $40-$65, complete in original box

Bugs Bunny 126 Cartridge Camera (1976)

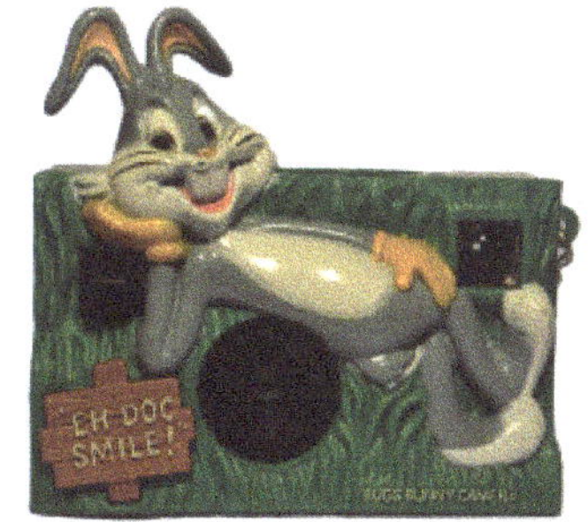

This is a 126 cartridge camera with a green plastic body and a large relief pattern of "Bugs Bunny" across the face. It uses "X-cubes" for flash. It was made in Hong Kong for Warner Bros. Inc., by Helm Toy Corp., under patent license from Eastman Kodak Co. You can expect fierce competition from Bugs Bunny/Looney Tunes collectors.

$20-$45, camera only; $50-$75 in original packaging

Cabbage Patch Kids 35mm Camera Outfit (2005)

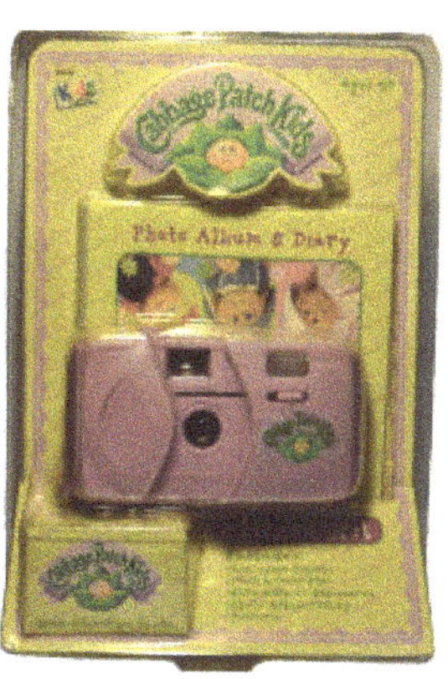

This is a higher quality 35mm camera than most "kids" cameras. The outfit comes with a 12-exposure roll of 35mm film, photo album and diary, and one AA battery (preloaded) to operate the flash. There is a sliding lens cover to protect the lens and viewfinder when not in use. The camera came in several colors and has a nice quality green "Cabbage Patch Kids" decal on the front. It has a simple one-click shutter and focus-free lens. This camera is sought after by both camera collectors and Cabbage Patch Kids collectors alike. It was manufactured 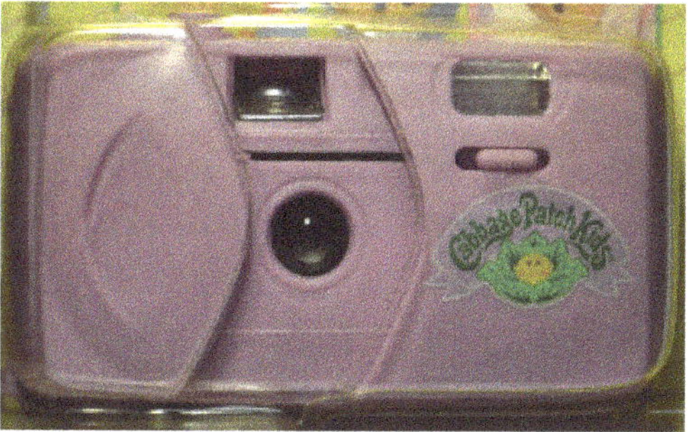 by Kids Only, Inc., MA, USA, and licensed by Original Appalachian Artworks, Inc., and made in China.

$5-$15, camera only; $15-$30, in original packaging

Cabbage Patch Kids 110 Camera (1983)

This camera is yellow with black trim on both the front and back. It uses 110 film cartridges and flip-flash bars. It has a green "Cabbage Patch Kids" logo on the front trim of the camera, with a simple one-click shutter and focus-free lens. It was made in China by Playtime Products Inc., New York, NY, USA, now a division of Tyco Toys, Inc. and parent Mattel, Inc. This camera is sought after by both camera collectors and Cabbage Patch Kids collectors alike.

$5-$15, camera only; $20-$40 in original packaging)

Cabbage Patch Kids 110 Camera (1985)

This camera is similar to the 1983 version and uses type 110 cartridge films. It has a simple one-speed shutter and focus-free lens and uses a flash bar for flash shots. Copyrighted by Original Appalachian Artworks, Inc., and made in China.

$5-$15, camera only; $20-$40, in original packaging

Cambridge Cigarette Single-Use Camera (1993)

This is an inexpensive plastic bodied camera with a cardboard wrap-around. Its red and white with "Cambridge" printed on the face, top, and sides and was a limited-offer premium if you purchased a carton of their cigarettes. The camera comes preloaded with 24 exposure, ISO 400, 35mm color print film. It also has a fixed-focus lens and one-click shutter; optical viewfinder and no flash. ©Philip Morris, Inc. and made in China by Concord Camera Corp., Avenel, NJ, USA. The Cambridge brand of cigarettes was first sold by Philip Morris Tobacco Co. in 1870 and is still sold in the United States and other countries.

$2-$12

Camel Smooth Shot Camera (1987)

This is a basic product camera that was offered as a premium to smokers with the purchase of a carton of Camel cigarettes. The camera is yellow and has the Camel logo on the left side of the viewfinder. The reusable camera uses standard 35mm roll films, and features a simple one-click shutter and focus-free lens. Camel cigarettes is one of many brands of the R.J. Reynolds Tobacco Company.[1] The camera was made in China.

$1-$10, camera alone; $5-$15 in original packaging

In 1987, R.J. Reynolds Tobacco Company celebrated the 75th anniversary of Camel cigarettes. The company based in Winston-Salem, NC, USA, was founded by R. J. Reynolds in 1874.

Canon Snappy '84 35mm Camera (1980)

This plastic special-edition 35mm camera with a flash was advertised as the "Official 35mm Camera of the 1984 Olympic Games" held in Los Angeles, CA, USA. It comes with a Canon 35mm, f/4.5 auto-focus lens and uses any standard 35mm roll-film. Original price was around $100. Copyrighted 1980 L.A. Olympic Committee and made in Taiwan by the Canon Camera Company. It is uncommon but not rare.

$20-$40, camera only; $50-$90 in original packaging

Care Bears Little Savers 110 Camera (1990)

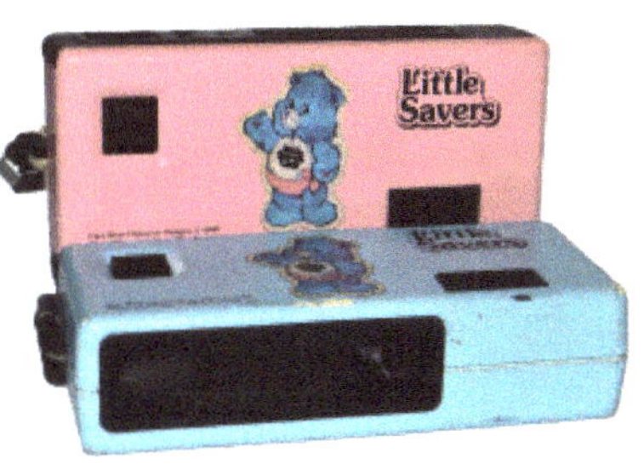

The Care Bears camera is available in two colors: blue or pink. The top of the camera has a sticker of a "Care Bear" in the center and "Little Savers" printed on the right behind the flash socket. It uses 110 film cartridges and flip-flash bars. Simple one-click shutter and focus-free lens. Made by the Concord Camera Corp., under license by American Greetings Corp., Cleveland, OH, USA, and distributed by General Mills, Inc., Minneapolis, MN, USA.

$20-$45, camera only; $25-$55 in original packaging

The Care Bears debuted in 1983 and accounted for $2 billion in sales within two years of their introduction.

American Greetings Corporation (founded:1906, incorporated:1944) also creates, markets, and licenses characters, including the Care Bears, Holly Hobbie, and Strawberry Shortcake.

Caterpillar 35mm "Creature Cameras" Camera (1986)

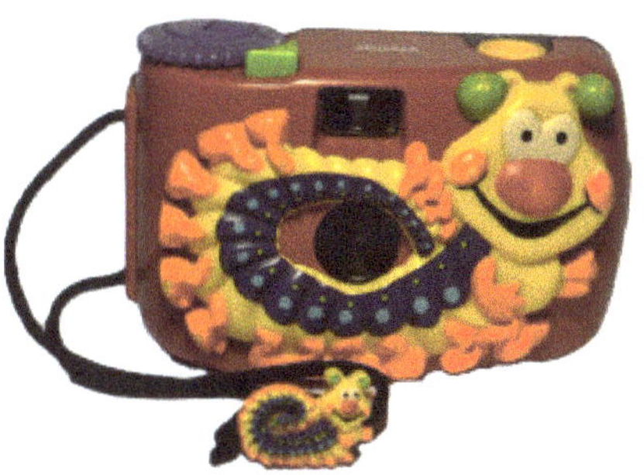

This camera is from the "Creature Camera" series by Kids Can Press and licensed by Provincial Products, Inc. It was part of their promotion of "Franklin the Turtle" book series and books about "Elliot Moose".

There is a large relief image of a Caterpillar on front of camera and a smaller caterpillar on the carry strap. Simple one click shutter and focus free lens and uses 35mm roll films. Flash models require two AAA batteries. Other "Creature Camera" series cameras include Franklin the Turtle, Batman & Robin, Polar Bear, Monkey, Cat & Mouse, Crocodile, Sesame Street, Rugrats, and famous Looney Tunes characters. It is manufactured in China by Vivitar Corporation; ©Provincial Products, Inc.; Uncommon.

$20-$50

Kids Can Press, Toronto, Ontario is a children's book publishing company.

The Caterpillar Disposable Camera Featuring Ward Burton (2002)

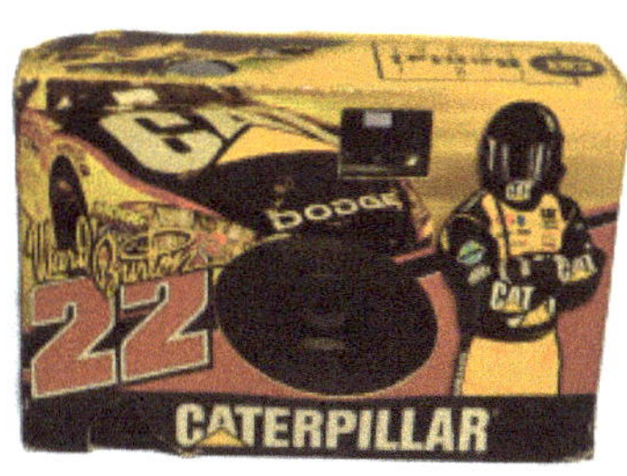

A cheap disposable plastic 35mm film camera with cardboard covering featuring Ward Burton (car #22) of Bill Davis Racing and used under license from Caterpillar, Inc., makers of heavy equipment such as bulldozers, backhoes, and mining equipment. It uses 12-exposure, ISO 400, 35mm color film (C-41). It was assembled in Mexico from Chinese and Japanese made parts and distributed by E–TOP–PICS, Inc.

$1-$10

Charlie the Tuna Camera (introduced 1971)

This is a camera made in good taste. It is large and made of plastic and molded and colored just as shown in the Starkist TV commercials featuring Charlie the Tuna during the 1960s and 1970s. It has a simple lens and shutter and used 126 cartridge film. A flashcube (requiring two AAA batteries) would be placed in the top of his beret he wears on his head for flash pictures. Additionally his name "Charlie" is also on top front of beret. A carry strap was included. The camera was available by mail order for $4.95 plus three StarKist tuna can labels. This camera was licensed by Starkist, Inc. and manufactured by Whitehouse Products Inc. USA.

$75-$150

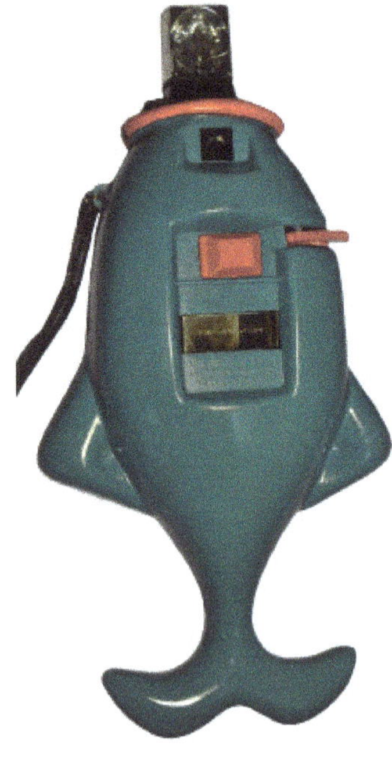

Whitehouse Products Inc. was a camera manufacturing company based in Brooklyn, NY., USA. They were founded in 1947 and were known for their Beacon style of camera and its many variations. Whitehouse and StarKist formed a partnership to produce the Charlie the Tuna novelty camera in 1971.

Clix-O-Flex TLR Novelty Camera (1947)

This is a twin lens reflex style novelty camera manufactured by Metropolitan Industries* of Chicago, Ill., and takes 16 - 1/2 frame photographs on No. 127 roll film. It has a 7.5mm, f/5 Maestar lens with simple single speed shutter.

$25-$50

About the only thing known about Metropolitan Industries is that they were makers of cameras during the 1940s. These cameras were a mix of designs and film sizes (which were usually type 120 or 127 roll-film). They did make an impressive list of camera models during their production years. These included the Capitol 120 & 127, Rival 120 Elite (basic metal box camera), Mirro-Flex, Pal Jr. (a box camera), Cardinal 120 (basic metal box camera), Metro-Cam & Metro-Flex, Clix-120 (basic metal box camera), Hamilton Super-Flex, and a long list of "Clix" cameras including the Clix-O-Flex.

Del Monte Chipmunks Camera (1992)

Features Alvin and The Chipmunks on the face of the camera and a Del Monte logo located beside the viewfinder. Camera strap is matching green and has The Chipmunks, Alvin, Theodore, and Simon, printed on it in black. Camera is black with a bright green front. Looks like a 35mm camera but uses type 110 cartridge film and there is a flash shoe on top. Simple one-click shutter and focus-free lens. Originally came in a box with instructions and a film processing mailing envelope. No film or flash comes with the camera. This was a mail away premium from Del Monte Foods Corp. Licensed by Bagdasarian Productions. It was made in China. Fairly common but a nice collectible.

$5-$15

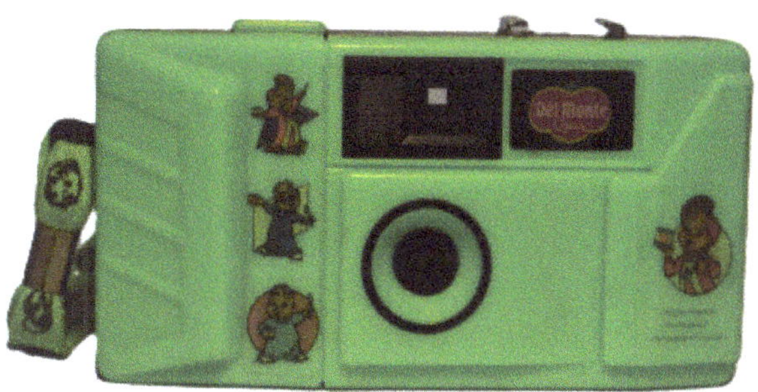

In 2004 Evergreen Concepts became the North American licensing agency for retro property Alvin and the Chipmunks. The Chipmunks are the most successful animated musical group of all time with over 43 million records sold.

Chipmunks 126 Camera (1960s)

Boxy plastic camera that has Alvin in heavy relief on face. He's dressed in all red and has a camera to "take" pictures too. "Smile" and "The Chipmunks" are written in red on the face. It uses 126 film cartridges and Magic-Cubes for flash. It was copyrighted by Bagdasarian Productions, Inc., and made in Hong Kong by Helm Toy Corp. It is uncommon.

$45-$80

Cinnamon Toast Crunch Camera (1992)

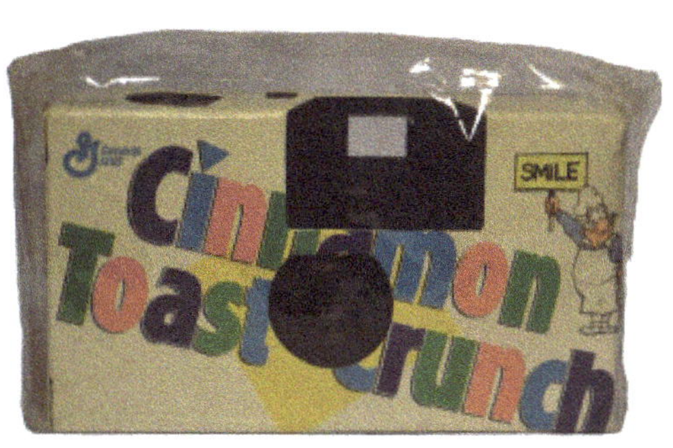

This is a cheap but nicely designed cardboard wrap-around disposable camera. This was a premium offered by General Mills, Inc., to promote their "Cinnamon Toast Crunch" cereal. It has no flash but comes preloaded with 24-exposure, ASA 400, 35mm color print film. No indication on the wrap where the camera was made or who made it but these type camera bodies usually are manufactured in China. The date of the camera could also mean it was made in Taiwan.

$2-$12, camera only; $15+ in original wrapper

General Mills promoted their cereal through many other avenues as well such as T-shirts, Hot Wheels, Mugs, Clocks, and Candles. They are one of the largest producers of cereals in the world.

CNBC Flash Camera (2000s)

This camera has a plastic body with colorfully designed cardboard covering. The logos of the National Broadcasting Company's cable networks CNBC and MSNBC along with the NBC's logo with its famous Peacock are printed on front. It comes preloaded with 35mm, ISO 400 color print film, and a battery to power flash. It has an easy one-click shutter and a 35mm, f/11 lens. Copyrighted by NBC Cable Network and made in China.

$2-$12

Coca-Cola Bear Camera (1999)

This is the 1999 edition of a Coca-Cola 35mm Collectible Camera and came packaged in a decorative tin. The original version of this camera was produced in the 1970s. The camera

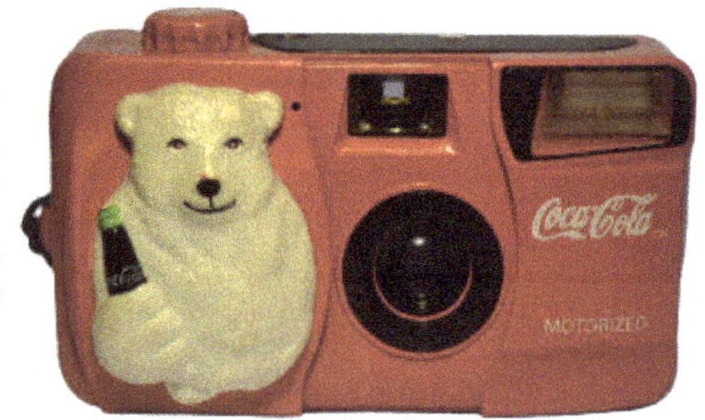

package came with a 35mm motorized wind and re-wind camera, a Coca-Cola pouch with a polar bear, film, batteries, and "Certificate of Authenticity." It has a simple one-click shutter and focus-free lens coupled with an auto sensor flash with "Red Eye" reduction. Licensed merchandise by Coca-Cola Co., and made in China. This camera is sought after by both camera and general Coca-Cola collectors. It is common.

$10-$20, camera only; $25-$45, complete kit with tin and Certificate of Authenticity

Coca-Cola Micro 110 Camera (1990)

This is a small micro 110 camera and keychain. The film canister itself makes up most of the body of the camera. It has a simple one-click shutter and fixed-focus f/8 lens. This camera is fiercely sought after by both mini keychain camera collectors and Coca-Cola collectors. It was made in Taiwan and licensed by The Coca-Cola Company, Inc. It is uncommon.

$80-$120

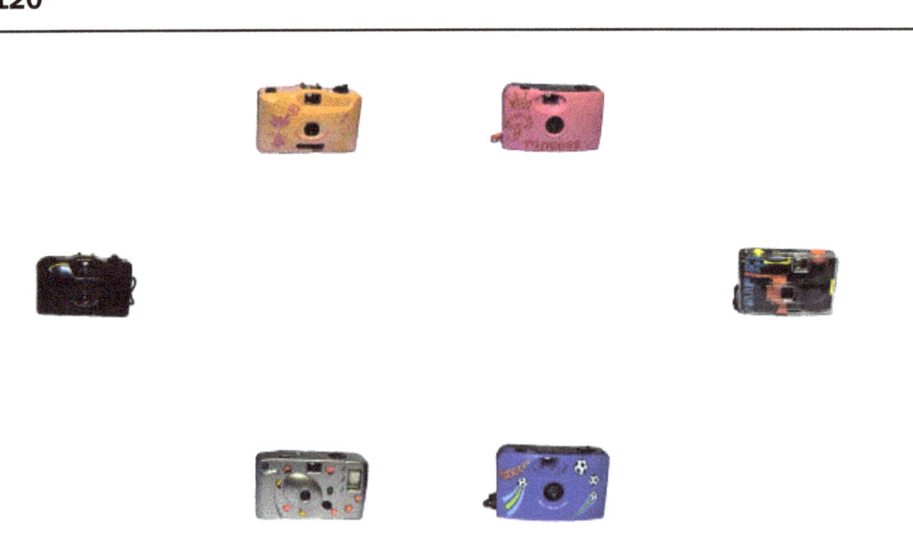

<u>**Crayola 110 Pocket Camera Outfit, Sport 35mm Outdoor Camera (1990s)**</u>

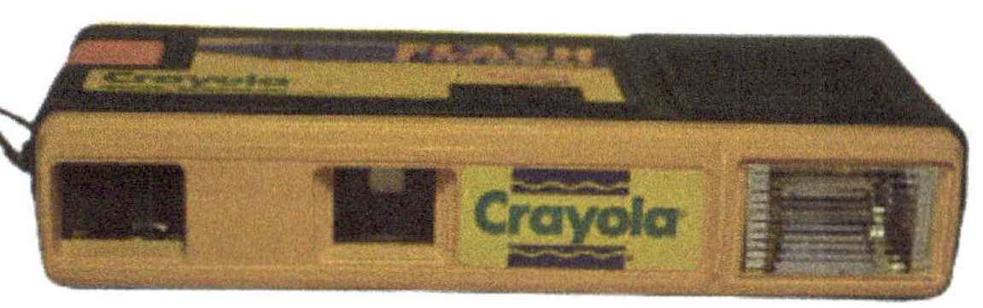

This Crayola camera was manufactured in China by Concord Camera Corp. of Avenel, NJ, USA, and is an officially licensed product of Binney & Smith Properties, Inc. This camera is green and yellow and has a built-in electronic flash. The outfit came with one roll of Scotch brand 12-exposure, ISO 200, 110 color film cartridge, and two AA batteries. The faceplate has "Crayola" printed on front with additional Crayola designations on top. It has a simple one-click shutter and focus-free lens. All versions can be commonly found. The 35mm Sport uses Kodak 400 film.

$1-$10, camera only; $10-$20 in original packaging

Hallmark Cards, Inc. bought Crayola, of Easton, PA, USA, in 1984. Crayola Co., became Crayola, LLC in 2007. Sakar International currently holds licenses for major brand franchises including Crayola. In October 2008 Concord Camera announced that it was going out of business.

Known as Peekskill Chemical Co., founded 1864 at Annsville, NY, USA, before becoming Binney & Smith, Inc., in 1902. Peekskill were makers of lamp black, charcoal, and red iron oxide paints and coatings used on barns and fencing as protection from the weather. In 1903, Binney & Smith sold their first Crayola crayons called "The Rainbow" (came eight in a box for a nickel). Paraffin is a by-product of petroleum refining and is non-toxic. Crayola uses this paraffin to make billions of their crayons each year. Peekskill Chemical operated well into the late 20th. century making yeast by-products under the Standard Brands name for the Fleischmann Company.

<u>**Crayola Sport 35mm (1990s)**</u>

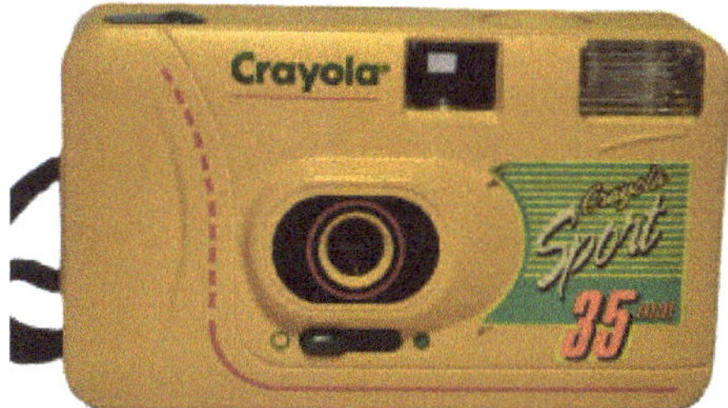

$1-$10, camera only; $10-$20 in original packaging

<u>**Cricket Lighter Camera (1990s)**</u>

This is a 35mm reusable plastic camera with an electronic flash. It has a 28mm focus free lens and simple one-click shutter operation along with an optical viewfinder and requires one AA battery to operate the flash. On the face is a picture of a cricket standing beside the words and logo "Cricket"; and just under states "The Safer Lighter." This example is yellow. Not sure if there are other colors or not. It is made in China and somewhat uncommon but not impossible to find.

$15-$30

the *Disney* section

Disney Cars 35mm Flash Camera Kit (2006)

This reusable 35mm point and shoot camera is equipped with a built-in electronic flash, and red in color with relief patterns on each side of the camera face. One has the No. 95 shown on it while the other is a picture of the "Red Car" with number "95" on the side. Top of the camera has the Cars logo. The kit has a camera, picture frame, one roll of Kodak UltraMax film, and one type AA battery. Also included is a camera strap with a car wheel attached to the end. Licensed by Global Point Products, LLC, Farmington, NY, USA,for Disney-PIXAR and made in China. Both collectors of Disney and cameras compete with each other for these cameras.

\$5-\$10, camera only; \$15-\$25 in original packaging

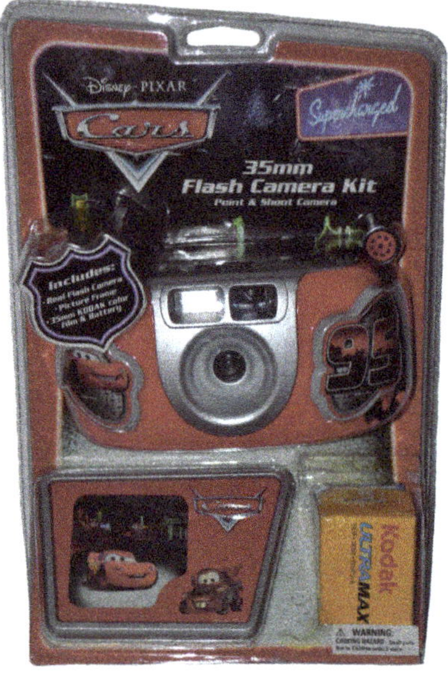

Disney Donald Duck Camera (1946)

Bakelite plastic camera that uses type 127 roll-films. It has a fixed-focus lens and simple 1/30-second leaf shutter but no flash. It has the words "donald duck" (in lowercase) arched around the top of the lens. On back in relief (embossed) is Donald and his three nephews Huey, Dewey, and Louie. The original camera design was done in an olive drab color (these are worth more). Original price of this camera was around \$2.98. Made by the Herbert George Company, Chicago, IL, USA, and commissioned and copyrighted by Walt Disney Productions, Inc.

\$30-\$50, camera only; \$170, in original packaging

More info: https://bit.ly/DonaldDuckCamera

Disney Donald Duck Head Camera (1950s, 1970s)

A plastic camera in the shape of Donald Duck's head. The eyes are used for the lens and the viewfinder. The shutter was activated by depressing his tongue. Both versions use type 127 roll-films (still available). Copyrighted by Walt Disney Productions, Inc., and made in Hong Kong. It is somewhat uncommon.

\$150-\$200 (1950s version)

\$120-\$140 (1970s version)

Disney's The Incredibles Camera (2004)

This camera was a promotional one to advertise the Disney/Pixar animated movie "The Incredibles" released in Nov. 2004 earning over $632M worldwide. It has a simple single-element plastic lens and one-click shutter operation and an optical viewfinder. Additionally, it comes preloaded with 27 exposures, ISO 200; 35mm color print film and has an electronic flash. It states on box that the film and lens was made in Germany. Camera made in the Czech Republic by Agfa-Gevaert AG, Mortsel, Belgium. ©Walt Disney Corp.; ©Pixar Animation Studios, Emeryville, CA. Pixar is known for their highly successful computer animated feature films.

$20-$30

More about Pixar here:

https://en.wikipedia.org/wiki/Pixar#Independent_company_(1986%E2%80%931999)

Info concerning The Incredibles animated movie: https://en.wikipedia.org/wiki/The_Incredibles

Disney Magic Selections Flash Camera (2008)

This is another plastic bodied camera with a wrap-around cardboard cover depicting Mickey Mouse, Minni Mouse, and Goofy cartoon characters holding Easter baskets in a country setting. A label is also present stating "Disney Magic Selections" on it. This ready-to-use disposable camera comes preloaded with 27 exposures, ISO 800; 35mm color print film and has an electronic flash. Simple one-click shutter operation, optical viewfinder, and focus free lens. It was distributed by Embassy International, Inc., Cincinnati, OH, USA. ©Walt Disney Productions, Inc. and made in China. It is common and there are other cameras to be found under the Disney Magic Selections label as well.

$12-$25

Disney Winnie the Pooh Camera (2008)

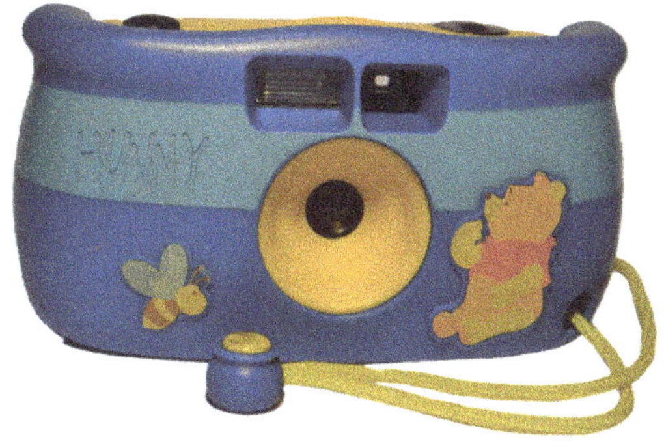

This was made for Fisher Price by Global Point Products, an authorized manufacturer of Disney licensed products. This is a 35mm ready-to-use point-and-click camera with manual film advance and a built-in flash for indoor use. It was also available without a flash. It uses 27-exposure, ISO 800 reloadable film cartridges available through Global Point Products. There is never any danger of ruining the film because rewinding was unnecessary. Kit included a photo frame, film, battery, and instructions. Camera features a wrist cord with a honey pot as the adjustment on the cord.

$5-$15 camera only; 50% more in original packaging

Disney Winnie the Pooh Single-Use Camera (2005)

A 35mm single-use camera with flash. Copyrighted by Walt Disney Productions, Inc., and made in China.

$2-$12

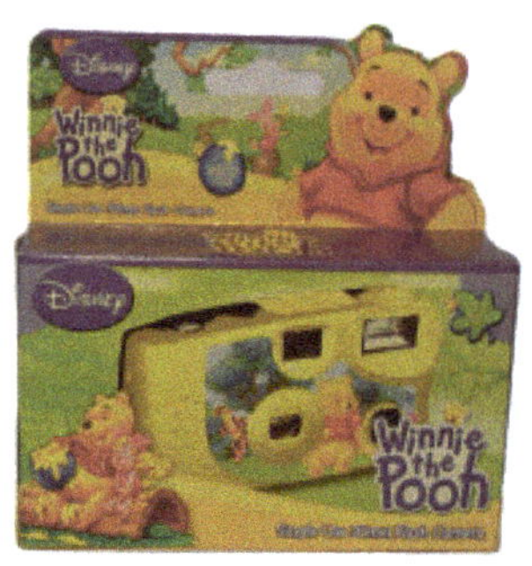

Dora the Explorer Camera and Radio Kit, Adventure Kit, Explorer Set, and the Big Adventure Kit (2012)

1. Camera and Radio Kit consists of 35mm reusable outdoor camera and AM-FM radio.

2. Adventure Kit consists of binoculars, flashlight, and 35mm reusable camera.

3. Explorer Set consists of binoculars, LCD watch, and 35mm reusable camera.

4. Big Adventure Kit has binoculars, flashlight, telescope, compass, and 35mm reusable camera.

$15-$30 all set/kit combinations.

©Viacom International, Inc. and made in China.

Dora the ExplorerCam (2012)

Single-use indoor-outdoor plastic camera with colorful sticker pictures of Dora and her monkey friend Boots with balloons and streamers. It comes preloaded with 27 exposure, ISO 400, 35mm color film and ready to use electronic flash. ©2012 Viacom International, Inc. and assembled in USA using foreign and domestic components.

$5-$15

Dora the Explorer Indoor-Outdoor Camera (2006)

This is a one-time use camera with colorful cardboard wrapping depicting Dora and her monkey friend Boots. Comes preloaded with 27 exposure, ISO 800, 35mm color print film, and ready to use electronic flash. ©2006 Viacom International, Inc. and assembled in USA.

$5-$15

Dora The Explorer is a series produced by Nickelodeon Animation Studio about the adventures of Dora (a Latina girl) and her buddy monkey Boots. Episodes aired on Nickelodeon from 2000 to 2014 and gave birth to a spin-off TV series called Go, Diego, Go! along with Dora and Friends: Into the City!, a TV sequel, as well as a live action feature film.

Dora The Explorer Outdoor Camera (2012)

Colorful re-usable plastic camera with Dora and her friend Boots depicted on its front. Uses standard 35mm roll films and has a flip-up view finder. No flash. ©Viacom International, Inc. and made in China.

$5-$15

Eastern Airlines Micro 110 Camera (1980s)

These small plastic cameras began showing up in the 1980s as cute little novelties to snap a photo with. The slightly better ones, like this one, had an actual body into which the 110 film cartridge would be placed. Many of these micro cameras were fitted with a fixed focus 20mm, f/11 lens and a 1/125 sec. mechanical shutter and pop-up viewfinder. This one was most likely a promotional hand-out for flying on Eastern Airlines and was also a promo for Pierre Cardin, a famous fashion designer, who sadly, passed away in 2020. It was made in China and is considered rare.

$80-$120

Eastern Air Lines operated from 1926, as a major airline player in the United States, until its demise in 1991; mostly due to labor disputes and a strike beginning in 1989 that finally did them in. Two of Eastern's competitors, American Airlines and Delta Air, each took over some of Eastern's routes. Eastern was located in Miami-Dade County, FL, USA.

Much more about Pierre Cardin here: https://en.wikipedia.org/wiki/Pierre_Cardin

Estes Snap-Shot Rocket Camera (1993-present)

This is probably one of the most, if not the most, unusual camera there is. The Estes SnapShot RTF (Ready to Fly) rocket and camera comes from the factory fully assembled and ready to launch. As the rocket soars to 500 feet high a color print photo is taken using a 110 cartridge camera housed in the nose cone of the rocket. (The film was Kodak Gold 110, 24-exposure, ISO 400 color-print film.)

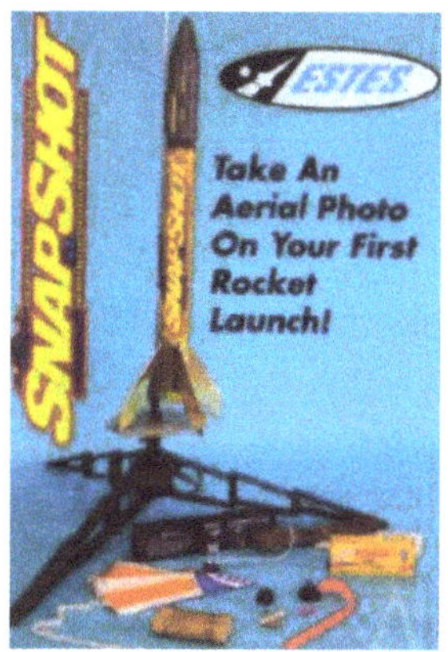

This all happens during the ejection stage of the flight at which point a 12 inch parachute is deployed to safely land the craft. The rocket is powered by a C6-5 single stage engine. Each time you launch the rocket the camera takes one photo so you would have to launch 24 times to use the entire roll of film.

Four AA alkaline batteries were needed to power the launch controller. Newer models use a digital camera to get the shot. A product of Estes-Cox Corp., Penrose, CO, USA, and made in China.

$25-$75

Estes-Cox Corp. was acquired by Hobbico, Inc. in January 2010. Estes also made the Estes Cineroc, an 8mm rocket camera that shot about 10 seconds of film, and the Estes Camroc rocket succeeded by the Estes Astrocam in 1977 and reintroduced in 2006 with new color schemes. The Estes website: https://bit.ly/EstesRockets

Fanta 35mm Camera (1990s)

This is an all orange plastic bodied camera with "Fanta" printed in blue on face. It has a focus free lens and simple one-click shutter operation, along with an optical viewfinder; no flash. It uses standard 35mm roll films and is reusable. ©The Coca~Cola Company; made in China; and is uncommon.

$5-$15

Fanta Can Shape Camera (2004)

This novelty camera is in the shape of a 375ml (12oz.) can of Fanta brand orange flavored soda. It was released in Australia as a part of a promotion of the Fanta brand soda drink; a trade mark of the Coca~Cola Company. Some features of the camera are an f/10, 28mm focus free lens, 1/100 sec. one-click shutter, and pop-up optical viewfinder; no flash. It uses 35mm roll films and is reusable. ©The Coca~Cola Company and made in China.

$20-$40

Fanta Single Use Camera (1995)

This is a cheap plastic box with a cardboard covering with "Your World Your Fanta" printed across face along with a stamp seal of some kind. The camera comes preloaded with 6 exposure, ISO 100, 35mm color print film; has a fixed focus-free lens; one-click shutter and optical viewfinder; no flash. This camera was used as advertising for the Fanta brand of orange soda pop. ©The Coca~Cola Company and made in China.

$2-$10

Fisher-Price 110 Camera (1984)

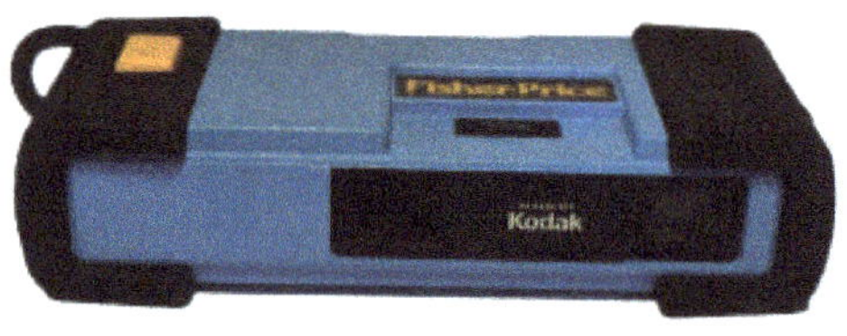

This camera was made by Kodak for Fisher-Price Toys and used 110 cartridge films. The body is blue in color with two large black bumpers on each side of the camera body. Tag on top states "Fisher-Price" while a tag on face states "Made by Kodak". The camera also has a fairly strong and long carry strap; simple fixed focus lens and one speed shutter; optical viewfinder. It's made in the USA by Eastman Kodak, Rochester, NY, USA

$10-$20

Fred Flintstone 126 Camera (1975)

This camera used 126 film cartridges and has large molded relief image of the cartoon character "Fred Flintstone" on front (a "Yogi Bear" version was also made). Shutter release is under Fred's nose and the lens is in his mouth. Simple one-click shutter and focus free lens; no flash. The original selling price was around $5 (USD). ©Hanna Barbera Productions Inc.* and made in Hong Kong.

$25-$35

In 1991, Hanna-Barbera (formed in 1944) was purchased by Turner Broadcasting System(owned by Ted Turner). In 1994, the company was renamed Hanna-Barbera Cartoons. In 1996, Turner Broadcasting merged with Time Warner. Today, the Hanna-Barbera name is only used to market properties and productions associated with Hanna-Barbera's "classic" works such as Huckleberry Hound, Yogi Bear, Snagglepuss, The Flintstones, and Scooby-Doo.

> **Collector's note:** Before the 126 cartridge models were made there were three 127 roll-film models made depicting Fred Flintstone, Huckleberry Hound, or Yogi Bear cartoon characters. **$12-$20**

Franklin the Turtle 35mm Camera (1986) and Other "Creature Cameras"

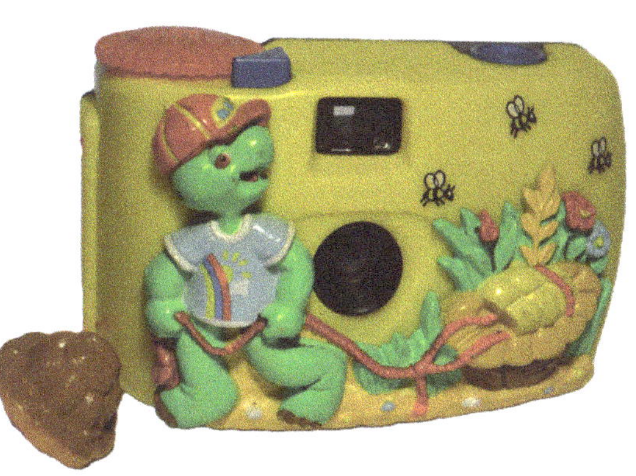

This camera is from the "Creature Camera" series by Kids Can Press and licensed by Provincial Products, Inc. It was part of their promotion of "Franklin the Turtle" book series and books about "Elliot Moose."

There are two versions of this camera either in yellow, without flash, or in blue, with flash. It has a large relief image of "Franklin the Turtle" on front of the camera and a turtle shell on the carry strap. It has a simple one-click shutter and focus-free lens, uses 35mm films and flash models require two AAA batteries.

Other "Creature Camera" series cameras include Batman and Robin, Polar Bear, Monkey, Cat and Mouse, Crocodile, Caterpillar, Sesame Street, Rugrats, and famous Looney Tunes characters. It was made in China by Vivitar Corporation. It is uncommon.

$20-$50

Kids Can Press, Toronto, Ontario, is a children's book publishing company.

As the story goes, Franklin finds a camera and wonders if he should try and find the owner or just keep it. Finders Keepers for Franklin (Print-Fiction). Bourgeois, Paulette and Clark, Brenda, illustrated. Kids Can Press (LRDC), 1997.

In November 2006, Vivitar Corporation (founded in 1938) was purchased by Syntax-Brillian Corporation. In August 2008, Sakar International of Edison, NJ, (founded in 1977) acquired Vivitar from Syntax-Brillian Corporation which then filed for bankruptcy that same year.

Freedom Family Zoom Camera by Minolta (1990s)

This 35mm camera has both auto film advance and a nice Minolta 35-60mm zoom lens. Other features include optical viewfinder, auto-focus, auto-exposure, and auto electronic flash with red eye reduction. It uses standard 35mm roll films and requires two type AA batteries to operate. It's made in Malaysia by the Minolta Company, LTD; now known as Konica-Minolta headquartered in Marunouchi, Chiyoda, Tokyo, Japan.

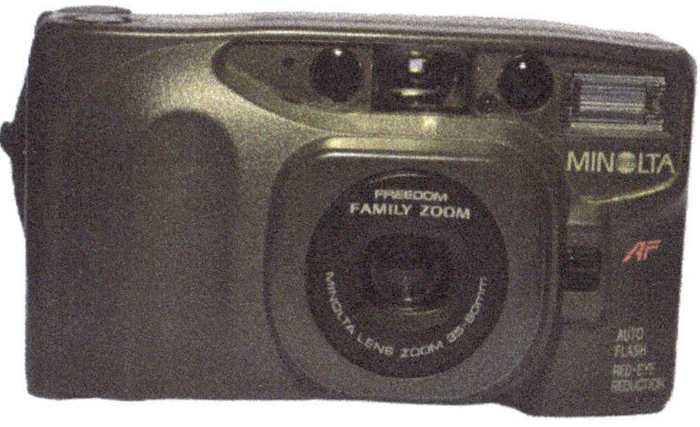

$20-$40

Konica and Minolta merged in 2003 and became Konica Minolta. Three years later Sony Corp. purchased the remaining camera interests in 2006.

More here: https://en.wikipedia.org/wiki/Konica_Minolta

Fun Pix Camera by Ansco (1980s-90s)

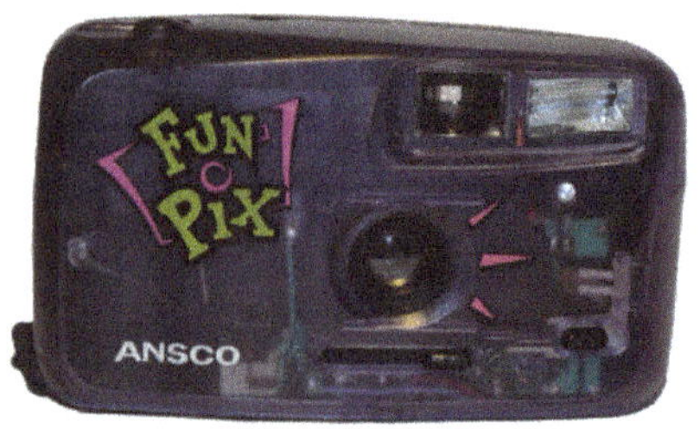

This plastic model came in various colors and is translucent so you can see the inner workings of the camera. The camera is reusable and uses 35mm roll films and sports a fixed-focus lens; simple shutter; optical viewfinder and electronic flash (requires two type AAA batteries). It was made in China by Ansco Photo Company, Binghamton, NY, USA.

$15-$30

the *Garfield* section

Garfield Single-Use Camera by 3M (1996)

This camera is a single-use type made of black plastic and half covered with a cardboard cover and came packaged in one of two box covers: blue or red depending whether the camera has a flash or not- the red box contained a camera without a flash and the blue box housed one with a flash. The camera cover itself is a white-to-yellow color and has "Garfield" printed below and to the right of lens along with the "3M" logo printed beside the optical viewfinder. This camera also came with its own unique "Gag" flap depicting Garfield thinking "Say Lasagna." It comes preloaded with 27 exposures, ISO 400, 3M brand 35mm color print film; electronic flash or not; preset fixed-focus lens and simple one click shutter. It's made in China for and by 3M Corp., St. Paul, MN, USA. ©PAWS, Inc.

$10-$20

Garfield Adventure Camera No.1 (2006)

This camera comes in blue plastic and is a talking camera. The front of camera has Garfield smiling in a cameo found just under the viewfinder and flash. On the opposite side is Garfield standing with "Party On!" printed just above him. The packaging states that this is number one in a series of talking cameras. Apparently the other cameras in the series were never made. The camera can be used indoors or out and has a sliding protective lens cover. It comes with batteries to power the electronic flash but no film; ISO 200 or 400, 35mm roll films are recommended. It was made in China by/for Akica Great Western Cameras, San Diego, CA, USA. ©PAWS, Inc.

This model is commonly found.

$30-60

Garfield Bootleg Camera (2023)

This is a 35mm plastic underwater camera that is a Bootleg made camera depicting Garfield the cat performing a magic act.

Value is undetermined.

Bootleg Garfield camera:

https://bootlegpals.tumblr.com/post/716573374740103168/bootleg-garfield-cam-era-source

Garfield Indoor Outdoor Camera (1990s)

This is a colorful reusable plastic camera that has a white front and black back. On the face find Garfield depicted in heavy relief, sticking out his tongue, found to the right of lens and under the viewfinder. Above lens find "Garfield" spelled out in colorful letters of orange, pink, and white. Uses type 35mm roll films; has a fixed focus lens; one-click shutter; optical viewfinder; and electronic flash. It is ©PAWS, Inc. and made in China; uncommon.

$25-$40

Garfield Outdoor Use Camera (2000s)

This is a reusable plastic camera that has a silver-gray front and a black back. On the face of camera Garfield the cat is depicted holding a camera. His name "Garfield" appears across the sliding lens cover. It uses 35mm films; has a pre-set fixed focus lens and one-click shutter; optical viewfinder; no flash. ©PAWS, Inc.

$15-$30

Garfield Single-Use Camera by Imation (1996)

This camera is a single-use type made of black plastic and half covered with a cardboard cover. The cover is a yellow-to-orange color with a wrap-around paw print and "watch the birdie!" printed just below and to the right of lens.

The cardboard cover has a flop-down "Gag" card with Garfield pictured with feathers hanging from his teeth and thinking "BURP!" to himself; probably to induce a smile while taking the shot. It comes preloaded with 27 exposures, System 800 35mm color print film and batteries to power the electronic flash; optical viewfinder; preset fixed-focus lens; simple one click shutter. It is made in China by Imation Corp., Oakdale, MN, USA. ©PAWS, Inc.

$10-$20

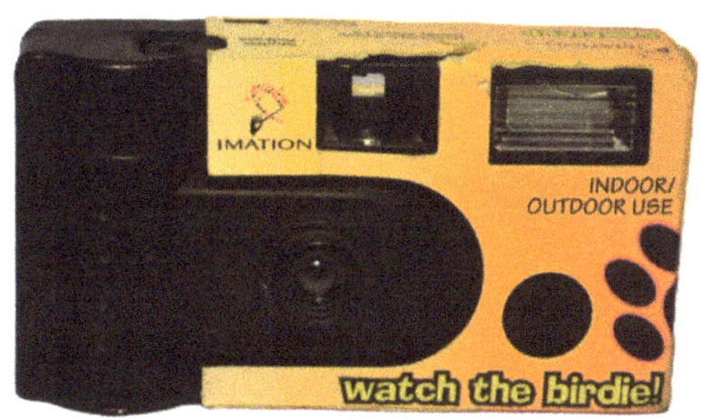

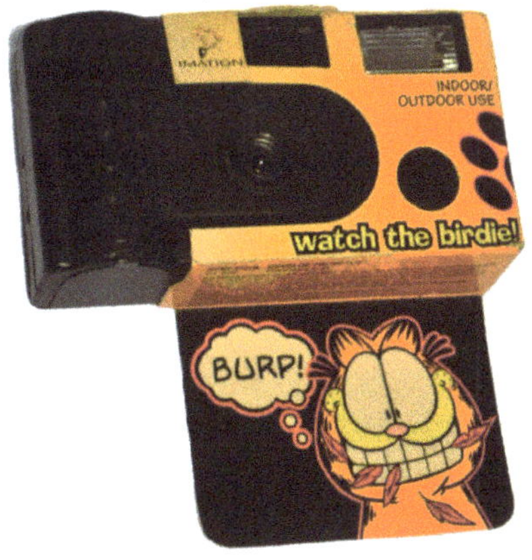

Garfield is a comic strip about the life of Garfield the cat, Odie the dog, and their owner Jon Arbuckle, first published in a local format in 1976, by creator Jim Davis. Garfield went on to national syndication starting in 1978. Paramount Global now owns PAWS, Inc. as of 2019. More here: https://en.wikipedia.org/wiki/Garfield

Ghost Hunting Camera (2006)

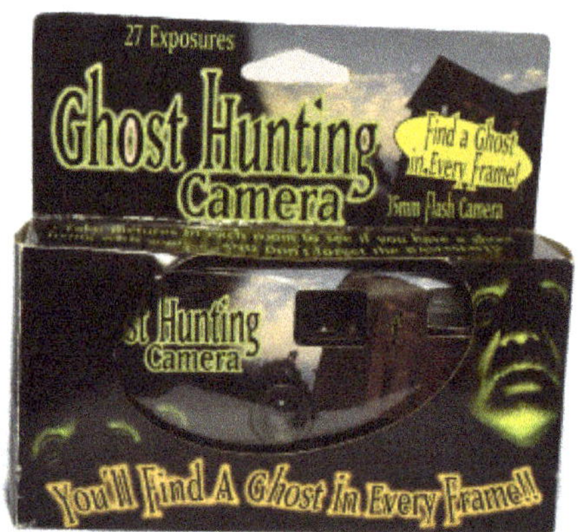

This is a plastic body with a cardboard covering depicting an old abandoned house with a ghost standing in one of the windows and stating "Ghost Hunting Camera" on face to left of the optical viewfinder. Upon taking pictures you "find a ghost in every frame" and "discover spooky images on your photos". It comes pre-loaded with 27 exposures; ISO 400; 35mm color print film; battery to power electronic flash; simple fixed focus lens and one speed shutter. It was made in China.

$30-$45

Go Bots 110 Camera (1984)

This is the same camera style as the Cabbage Patch Kids 110 camera. It is gray with black front and red back trim and has the "Go Bots" sticker on the face. It uses 110 film cartridges and flip-flash bars and features a simple one-click shutter and focus-free lens. It was made in China by Playtime Products Inc., New York, NY, USA, now a division of Tyco Toys, Inc., and parent Mattel, Inc.

$12-$20 camera only; $40-$75 in original packaging

Halloween Camera by Photo Expressions (2000)

This fun single-use 35mm flash camera was made in 2000 and manufactured by Elite Brands, Inc., under license from Polaroid Corp. Each photo has one of six messages ghoulishly printed into each picture for the kids' delight. There is Halloween Surprise, Ghosts, Goblins and Witches, Trick or Treat, Booooo!, Ghouls Night Out, and Fright Night. It has a simple one-speed shutter and pre-set plastic lens and was made in China. It is somewhat uncommon.

$10-$20

Hannah Montana Single-Use 35mm Flash Camera (2008)

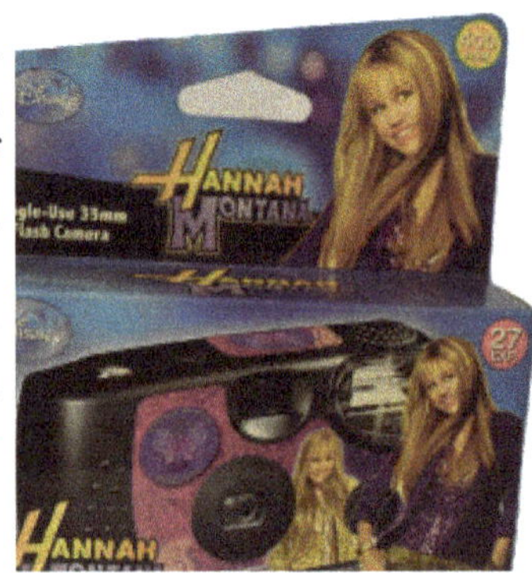

This boxed single-use camera is a basic black camera with a black body and decorative sticker on the face depicting Hannah Montana. It features "Dual Flash Modes" offering a choice of "continuous mode" or "single-flash mode." It comes preloaded with a roll of 400 ASA, 27-exposure, 35mm color print film. This camera was offered through a special deal between Walgreen's stores and Disney. Licensed by Disney, it was made in China. Collectors of both cameras and Hannah Montana collectibles compete to obtain this camera.

$5-$15

Hannah Montana is an American television series that debuted on March 24, 2006.

Hardee's French Fry Camera (1998)

This is an odd plastic camera in the shape of a blue bag of golden French fries and has "Hardee's" name and logo printed above lens. The Pepsi Cola logo is also present on lower right face. It has a Meniscus 28mm, f/11, fixed focus lens, single-speed shutter, and optical viewfinder; and uses 35mm roll films with ISO 200 or 400 recommended. No flash. It was made in China by Ginfax, Hong Kong, and marketed by Simon Marketing, Int., based in Gloucester, MA, USA.

$25-$50

Harvard Museum 35mm Flash Camera (2016)

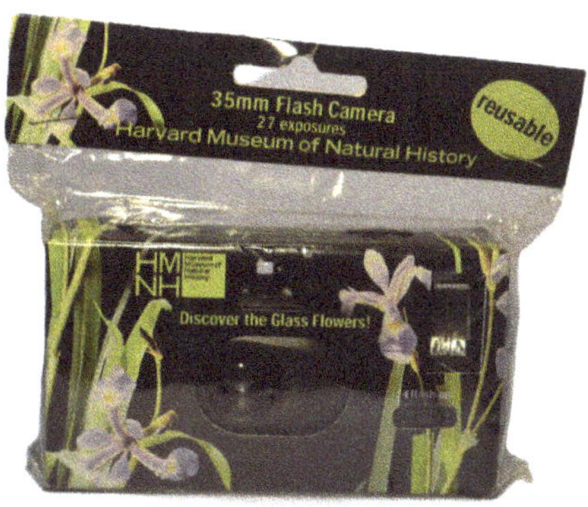

On the packaging it states that this camera is reusable. The body of camera is black color plastic with a cardboard covering depicting an Iris versicolor flower on face and a Dahlia pinnata on back. To reuse the camera, it will become necessary to remove the cardboard cover to access the film compartment. This camera was part of a promotion of the Glass Flowers Collection at the Harvard Museum of Natural History located at 26 Oxford Street, Cambridge, MA, USA. It comes preloaded with 27 exposures; 35mm color print film; battery; has a fixed focus lens; simple shutter; optical viewfinder; and electronic flash. It's made in China for the Neato Products Company, LLC, located in Scottsdale, AZ, USA.

$5-$15

More info about the glass flowers here: https://en.wikipedia.org/wiki/Glass_Flowers

Hello Kitty 35mm Flash Camera Kit (2008)

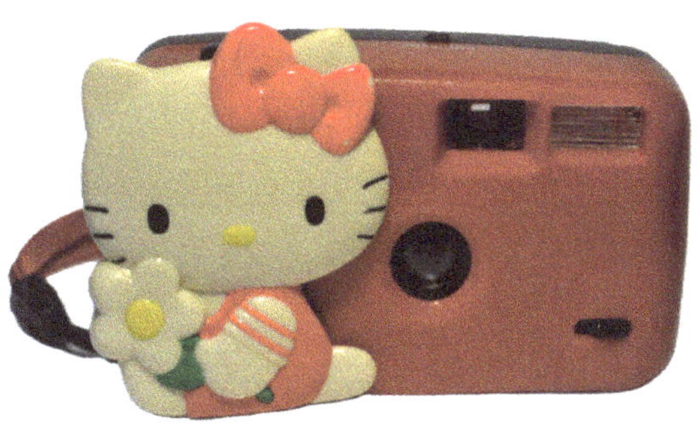

This 35mm flash camera was made as a collectible and came with manual film advance and rewind, strap with a charm, Hello Kitty photo frame, one roll of Kodak 12-exposure, ISO 400, 35mm film, and one Kodak AA battery. The kit also comes with a one year guarantee. Made by Global Point Products under license from Sanrio Company, Ltd., who holds the copyright, as an authorized manufacturer, wholesaler and supplier of Hello Kitty products. In addition to camera collectors, collectors of Hello Kitty products will compete for this unit.

$5-$15, camera only; $15-$35 in original packaging

Hello Kitty 35mm Flash Camera (1997)

This is a pink plastic bodied camera with the character Hello Kitty pictured on face to left of lens. The camera itself is an Epion model made by Fujifilm and has a Fujinon lens; optical viewfinder; and electronic flash. It uses standard 35mm roll films with ISO 200 or 400 recommended; made in Japan by Fuji for ©Sanrio Corp., Tokyo, Japan.

$20-$40

Hello Kitty Camera by Polaroid I-Zone (2000)

This Polaroid version of a Hello Kitty camera produces small (36mmx24mm) images on Polaroid Pocket Film. The Camera was sold as a complete kit and included a six-exposure film pack and two AA batteries to power the built-in electronic flash (unlike other Polaroid integral films, this new Pocket Film does not contain its own power source).

In addition to standard prints, a special film is available to allow the camera to produce small photographic stickers as well. It has a simple one-click shutter and focus-free lens. Hello Kitty is a licensed product of the Sanrio Co., Ltd., and made by Polaroid Corp. The I-Zone camera was introduced in 1999 and was originally available in a choice of three bright colors: vibrant green, red, and blue.

$5-$15

Sakar International currently holds licenses for major brand franchises including Hello Kitty.

Sanrio marketed Hello Kitty on nearly every product imaginable. The Hello Kitty character was first introduced in 1974 and now rivals Mickey Mouse. By 2000, Sanrio had placed the Hello Kitty character on more than 15,000 products, including cameras!

Polaroid was purchased by the capital firm One Equity Partners in 2002 who filed bankruptcy in 2008. PLR IP Holdings LLC, Minnetonka, MN, USA, now controls the Polaroid brand name.

Hello Kitty Fisheye Camera (2010)

This reusable plastic camera is red, white, and blue color themed and has the Hello Kitty character's face located to the left of the lens and under the electronic flash. Just under the lens it states "The first 35mm fisheye camera of the world". Hello Kitty is also found on the back of the camera with a camera in her hands- err paws. The lens features a 170 degree "wide eyed perspective" of your photos field of vision and has a red plastic lens cap that reads "Hello Kitty" molded into the cap.

The lens aperture is f/8 coupled with a 1/100th sec. speed shutter; optical viewfinder; and any standard 35mm roll film can be used with ISO 200 or 400 recommended; requires one type AA battery for the flash; carry strap. It is made in China for Lomography.com under license ©1976, 2010 Sanrio Co. LTD, Tokyo, Japan.

$40-$80 camera alone; $150-$200 complete in original box.

Lomography has a complete line of fisheye cameras that come in several different colors. You can meet the entire family including the Hello Kitty Fisheye camera here: https://www.thelomographer.com/2010/nl_hello_kitty_fisheye/

He-Man 110 Camera (1985)

This is a most interesting designed camera in the form of a castle; Castle Grayskull, with its mouth forming the doorway into it. He-Man stands to one side with his ax in hands; all in heavy molded relief. This Masters of the Universe camera used type 110 film cartridges and X-type flash cubes. Original selling price was $14.99. It was produced by HG Toys, LTD., Long Beach, NY, USA. ©Mattel, Inc. and made in China.

$75-$150 camera alone; $200-$300 in original packaging.

> **Collector's note:** A pink (Crystal Castle) "She-Ra Princess of Power" camera was also released in 1985.

Hi-Color Micro 110 Camera (1980s-90s)

These small plastic cameras began showing up in the 1980s as cute little novelties to snap a photo with. The slightly better ones had an actual body into which the 110 film cartridge (available with either 12 or 24 exposures) would be placed. The cheaper ones, like this one, used the 110 film cartridge as the body of the camera and simply snapped into place. Many of these micro cameras were fitted with a fixed focus 20mm, f/11 lens and a 1/125 sec. mechanical shutter. None have a flash. This one was made and sold in Argentina, South America and is uncommon.

$10-$20 camera alone; $40-$65 in original unopened packaging.

Hit Type Novelty Cameras (1947-1960s)

This class of novelty subminiature cameras is commonly referred to as "Hit Types" because it was one of the first and most popular of names for this type of camera. The basic book value for most Hit Type cameras is **$20-$30**. Although they all appear to be the same, each different model has its subtle differences. Most have black leatherette and chrome bodies with various model names, while other models have gold metal and/or colored leatherette. These more colorful touches add another $12-$20 to the book value. Recent and more common models are the lowest priced at $12-$20 while the uncommon names command $30-$50.

Hollywood Camera (2004)

This camera with a plastic body has a wrap-around cardboard cover and "Hollywood Flash Camera" printed on the front. This is a single-use camera and comes preloaded with 27-exposure, ISO 400, 35mm color print film as well as the batteries to power the flash. It was also available without a flash. It was made in China.

$5-$15

Hollywood Oscars Single-Use Camera (2010)

This camera comes preloaded with a 27-exposure, ISO 400, 35mm color print film and battery to power the electronic flash. It was made in China.

$5-$15

Hot Wheels 35mm Flash Camera 4 Piece Kit (2005)

This is a reusable 35mm flash camera that features a Hot Wheels car on a colorful face along with the Hot Wheels logo beside the optical viewfinder. The kit includes a 35mm camera, 12 exposures, ISO 400 35mm color film, one type AA battery to power flash, and photo album. A carry strap is also included. Manufactured for and distributed by KID-designs, Inc., Rahway, NJ, USA. ©2005 Mattel, Inc.; and made in China.

$15-$30 complete kit; $5-$15 camera only

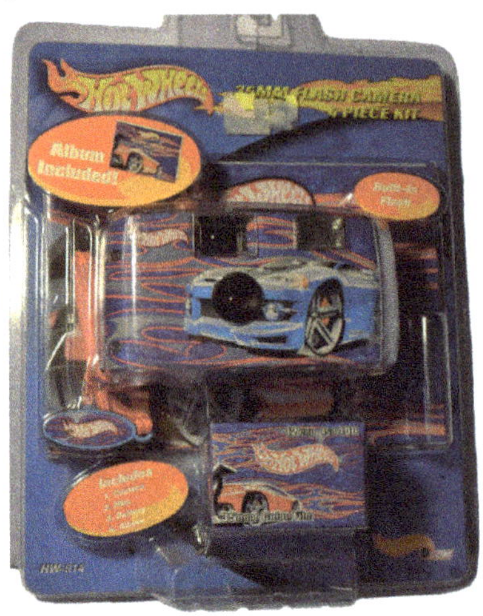

Hulk Hogan 110 Camera (1991)

This is a pocket camera with a Hulk Hogan figurine mounted on the front. It uses type 110 cartridge films and has an electronic flash requiring two AA batteries to operate. It has a focus-free lens and one-click shutter. It features a "Hulk Hogan's COLOR imprint on every photo." The camera originally sold for $12.99 at Toys-R-Us toy stores. It was copyrighted by TitanSports, Inc., licensed by Marvel, Inc., and made in China.

$20-$40, camera only; $85-$105 in original packaging

Hulk Hogan, real name Terry Gene Bollea, is a highly recognized wrestling star and is regarded to be one of the greatest professional wrestlers of all time. https://bit.ly/Hulk-HoganWiki

Hysteric Glamour Mini Camera (2006)

This unique camera is made to look like someone with a red mask on their face while also sticking out their tongue. The camera wasn't for sale so it's assumed it was a handout to kids for entertainment/advertising purposes. It has a 35mm, f/11 lens, and 1/100th sec. shutter speed; optical viewfinder and electronic flash. The camera uses any standard 35mm roll films with ISO 100, 200, and 400 being the recommended film speeds to use; uncommon.

©2006 Hysteric Glamour Mini, Japan, and made in China. Hysteric Glamour is a Japanese fashion designer label created in 1984 by artist Nobuhiko Kitamura.

$40-$50 camera alone; $60-$100 in original blister packaging.

More about Hysteric Glamour here: https://en.wikipedia.org/wiki/Hysteric_Glamour

Hysteric Glamour web site: https://www.hystericglamour.jp/

Impulse Voltron Starshooter 110 Camera (1985)

This instamatic type camera was made during the Transformer craze that peaked around the mid 1980s. A "Transformer" is a toy that can be switched between two forms. In this case one is a robot-like character while the other can be something else such as a tank, helicopter, truck, ship, or camera, for example. This "Transformers" knock-off can be either the powerful robot, "Voltron," or what looks like a 35mm camera, which actually is a 110 camera and uses the 110 film cartridges.

It has a simple one-click shutter, focus-free plastic lens and uses flashcubes. "Starshooter" is printed on the camera and it originally sold for $26.95, it was made in Macau (China) under license by Impulse. Ltd. Located in Missouri, USA, Voltron is a registered trademark of World Events Productions, St. Louis, MO, USA.

$65-$90

The Transformers toy line was developed by Hasbro, Inc., and Takara Co., Ltd., Japan in 1983 and were introduced into the U.S. marketplace in 1984.

The Voltron robot was first featured in the 1980s animated television series "Voltron: Defender of the Universe."

World Events Productions is a U.S. animation and distribution company.

Incredible Hulk Camera (1978)

This is a 126 cartridge film camera that is of the same design as the Spider-Man camera of the same year. However, this one depicts The Incredible Hulk character. Flash cubes are used for flash pictures and it has a focus-free lens. It was produced by Vanity Fair and made in Hong Kong.

$25-$45, camera only; $55-$100 in original packaging

The Incredible Hulk superhero character is a comic book published by Marvel Comics, Inc. The character was first published in 1962 and went on to inspire TV shows and movies, video games, merchandise and collectible items. Find more information about The Incredible Hulk here: https://bit.ly/IncredibleHulkComic

Iron Man Message Camera (2008)

This is another cheap generic disposable camera with a cardboard wrap-around. This one depicts Iron Man, the super hero featured in Marvel Comic books, TV, and movies.

This 35mm single-use camera comes with a flash and 18-exposure, ISO 400, 35mm film. Each photo prints with a message from Iron Man on it. It has a simple one-click shutter and focus-free lens. It originally sold for $7.99 and was made in China for Marvel Studios and Paramount Pictures and licensed by Sakar International.

$5-$15

Sakar International is the holder of licenses for major brand franchises including Iron Man and Spider-Man, The Incredible Hulk, Star Wars, LeapFrog, Jeep, Hello Kitty, Crayola, and Made for iPod and For Dummies.

i Scream GoGoCam (2003)

These two examples feature an ice cream bar on a stick on one and a cool refreshing snow cone on the other. There are other designs and colors to look for. These are ready to use [generic] cameras and come preloaded with 27 exposures, ISO 800, 35mm color print film (film made in Italy). A battery is included to power the electronic flash. ©2003 Target Brands, Inc. and distributed by Target Corp., Minneapolis, MN, USA; and made in China.

$1-$10

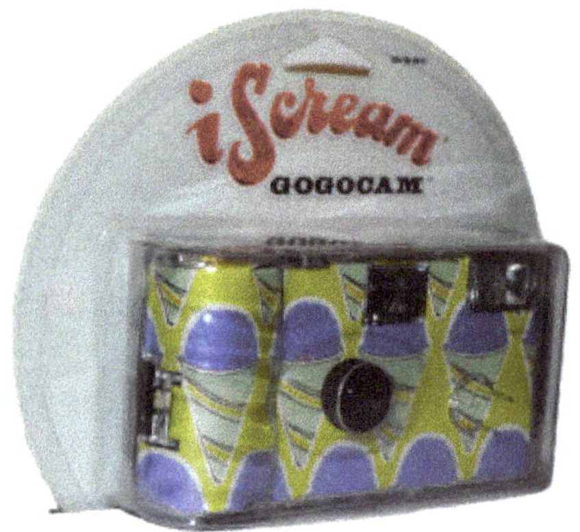
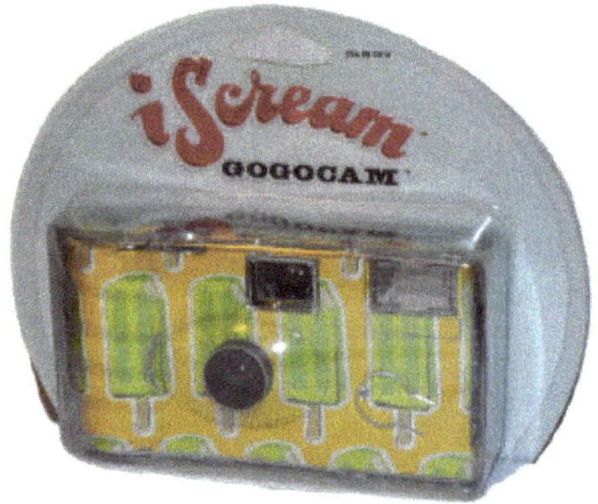

iZone 200 Camera by Polaroid (2004)

This version of Polaroid's iZone cameras were marketed to children and came in various colors and designs. The camera was sold in fancy miniature lunch boxes. It used 12 exposures Pola-

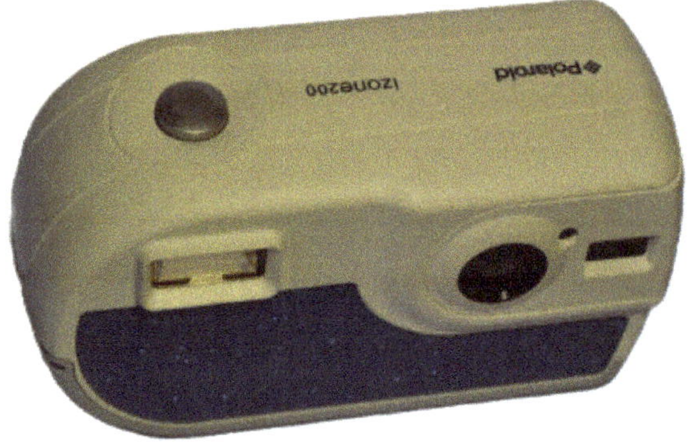

roid iZone 200, ISO 640 instant films, which were different from the I-zone models made in 1999. Other features include auto electronic flash (requires two type AAA batteries), auto focus; and optical viewfinder; carry strap. It was made in China and assembled in the Netherlands for Polaroid Corp.; films are no longer available; ©2004 Polaroid Corp., Waltham, MA, USA; common.

$20-$40

I-Zone Cameras and Special Markets I-Zone by Polaroid

Introduced in 1999, the Polaroid I-Zone cameras are in a flurry of colors including pastels and translucent models. These cameras use a special Polaroid instant "Pocket Film." Although the picture size is the same as that of 35mm film (24x36mm), not regular 35mm films. The films for the I-zone models were discontinued in 2006.

Other features were a focus-free lens, a built-in selectable flash, and manual film advance. The power source is two AA batteries unlike so many of the Polaroid cameras made just before that had the power source built-in to the film pack. It was copyrighted by Polaroid Corp., Inc., and some standard models were made in Thailand, others made in China.

$2-$12, standard models

<u>**I-Zone Cameras and Special Markets I-Zone by Polaroid, continued**</u>

Several special markets I-Zone models were produced and include:

Bugs Bunny, Barbie, Pokemon, American Girl, Hello Kitty, Tweety Bird, a "Millennium Silver" edition (a standard I-Zone camera in silver in 2000), and the Radio camera. These cameras, among other Polaroid models, were intended for "Special Markets" distribution which included prizes and give-aways, corporate premiums, and non-retail distribution. These models were actually manufactured for Polaroid by Tomy, a Japanese toy maker.

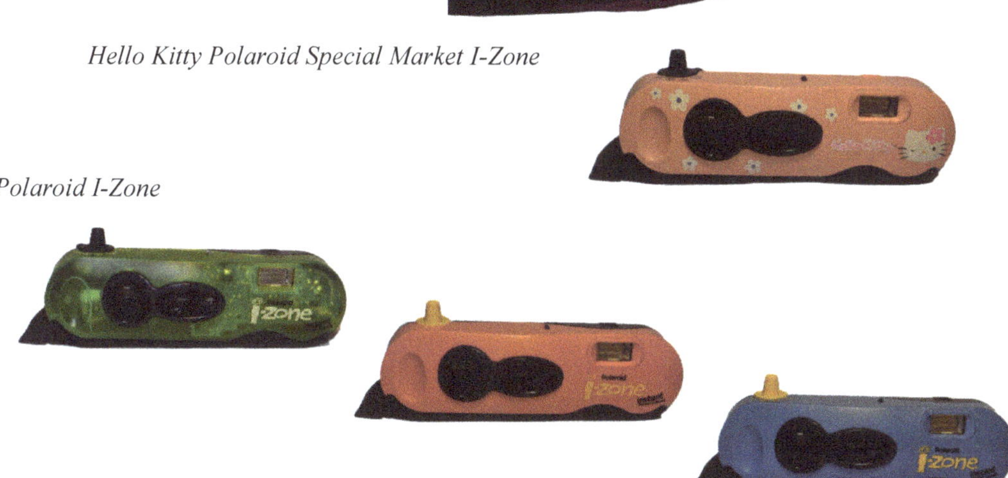

Barbie Polaroid Special Market I-Zone

Hello Kitty Polaroid Special Market I-Zone

Polaroid I-Zone

$50-$150+, special markets models

<u>Japanese Kawaii 110 Camera (1985)</u>

This is a cute (Kawaii) plastic camera that features animated cartoon characters expressed in the Kawaii form of Japanese art, a large part of their pop art culture. Simple loading of the 110 film cartridge and one-click shutter operation makes this camera easy to use. No flash. It is made in Japan by Bandai Company, LTD., Tokyo, Japan; a multinational manufacturer and distributor of toys.

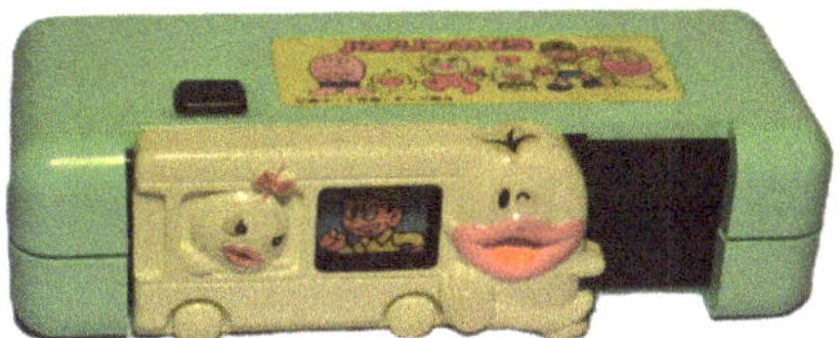

$40-$60

More about Kawaii Japanese art here:

https://en.wikipedia.org/wiki/Kawaii#:~:text=Illustrator%20Rune%20Naito%2C%20who%20produced,culture%20and%20aesthetic%20of%20kawaii.

Jazz 207 Point and Shoot Camera (1997)

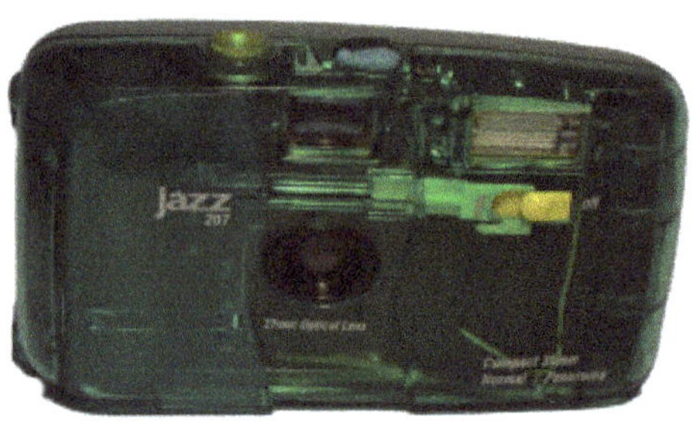

Cheap plastic reusable camera that shoots either normal or panorama pictures. It has a focus-free 27mm, f/9.5 lens, shutter speed 1/100 second, and an electronic flash that requires one AA battery for flash. It uses standard 35mm films and comes in various colors of translucent or "Jellies." It was made in China and distributed by Jazz Photo Corp.

$25-$45

Note: There are many other cameras with the Jazz name. Some are reusable while others are single-use.

Jazz Juicy Indoor-Outdoor Camera (2004)

A plastic single-use camera that came in various colors, this one is the Tangerine Begonias. The word "Juicy" is printed just below the flash. Comes preloaded with 27-exposure, ISO 400, 35mm color print film, as well as the battery to power the electronic flash. Shutter speed is 1/100 seconds and it has a 25mm focus-free Japan optics lens. It was made in China.

$5-$15, camera only; $20-$40, in original packaging

Johnson's Baby Camera (1990s)

A plastic camera with cardboard covering with "Johnson's Baby" printed on the face along with other things like rattles and balls. The camera is a promotion for Johnson's Baby powder. It comes preloaded with ISO 400, 35mm color print film with a simple shutter and lens but no flash. Copyrighted by Johnson & Johnson, Inc., and made in China.

$1-$10

Jonas Brothers Single-Use Camera (2000s)

A plastic camera with colorful cardboard wrap-around cover that depicts the Jonas Brothers on stage. The box declares, "Puts YOU in the picture with the Jonas Brothers." The camera has an electronic flash and comes preloaded with 24-exposure, ISO 400, 35mm film and battery to power flash. Copyrighted by Walt Disney, Inc., and made in China.

$10-$20

Just Ducky Character Camera (1999)

This camera body is designed to look like a classic bathtub rubber duck. It uses 35mm rollfilms, is reusable, and has a focus-free lens but no flash. Copyrighted by Department 56, Eden Prairie, MN, USA, and made in China.

$40

Kellogg's Corn Flakes 110 Keychain Camera (1990)

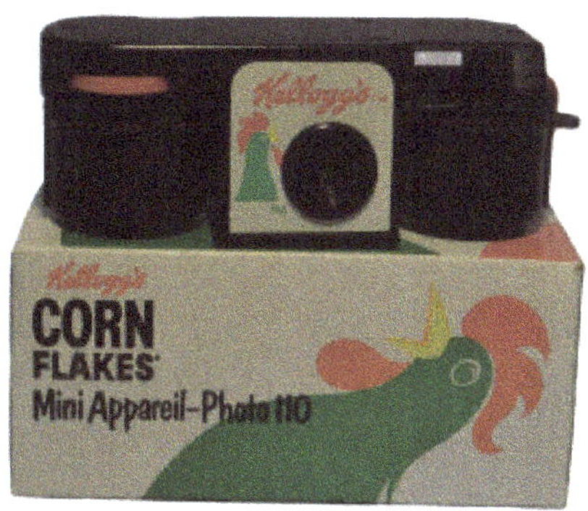

This micro 110 camera/key chain combination depicts the Kellogg's Rooster next to the lens as well as the Kellogg's trademarked text and was part of a advertising promotion between 1989 and 1990. The price was $4.95 and two box tops from any Kellogg's products. The film canister itself makes up most of the body of the camera. It has a simple one-click shutter and focus-free lens. It came packaged in a box with the Kellogg's Corn Flakes Rooster printed on it and instructions. It was made in Taiwan. It is fairly common despite its age.

$5-$15, camera only; $20-$30 in original packaging

Kellogg's Pop-Tart Camera (2007)

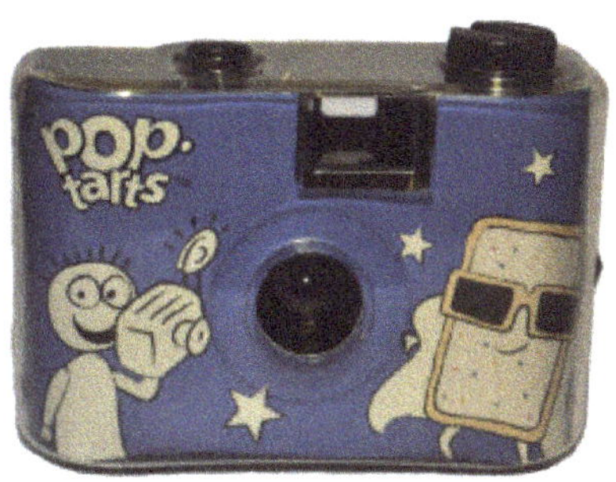

This 35mm camera was a premium offered on the Kellogg's Pop-Tart box and features a blue cardboard camera cover with "Pop-Tarts" printed on the front and two character drawings, one is a sunglass-wearing Pop-Tart and the other a character with a camera in hand. It has a simple one-click shutter and focus-free lens. It was made in China under license for Kellogg NA Co., Battle Creek, MI, USA.

$1-$10

Kellogg's Cereal Disposable Camera (2005-2007)

This was one of three theme-cameras used as promotional premiums for Kellogg's cereal products. It is a cheap disposable plastic body with no flash and a cardboard wrap-around covering that came with a 24-exposure 35mm film depicting either Tony the Tiger from the Frosted Flakes, Toucan Sam from the Fruit Loops, or the Snap, Crackle, and Pop characters from the Rice Krispies cereal boxes. The camera was free in a box of cereal, no need to collect points or box-tops or mail anything in to claim. It was made in China for Logistix Limited.

Kellogg's also gave away Pop-Tart-themed cameras so look for them as well.

- Fruit Loops Disposable Camera
- Tony the Tiger Disposable Camera
- Snap, Crackle and Pop Disposable Camera

$1-$5

Kentucky Fried Chicken Camera (1990s)

This is an all red plastic camera with a black back and green controls. It features a graphic outline image of Colonel Harland Sanders on the lower front with "Kentucky Fried Chicken" trademark words beside his picture. It uses 35mm roll films and there is no built-in flash but has a hot-shoe for an electronic flash. It was made in China.

$15-$30

KFC Camera (1990s)

This plastic camera is available in several colors and has a sticker that reads KFC on one side and an image of Colonel Harland Sanders on the other. It uses 35mm film and has a f/4 lens with a 1/250 shutter. The recommended film is ISO 200. It is common and made in China.

$10-$20

KFC Chicky Club Camera (1990s)

Yellow plastic camera with "KFC Chicky Club" and a chicken giving two thumbs up on its face. It uses 35mm films, but has no flash. It was made in China.

$12-$25

KFC Colonel Sanders Camera (1997)

This is a red plastic camera with black back that depicts Colonel Sanders in heavy relief on lower face wearing a little pointed hat and three stars above the lens: pink, yellow, and blue. On the back, KFC is printed in the lower right corner. It uses ISO 400, 35mm roll films. There is no flash, but it has a hot-shoe for one. Copyrighted 1997 by AST Company, LTD. It was made in China.

$20-$35, camera only; $45-$65, in original packaging

Klutz 35mm Camera (2001)

The Klutz 35mm camera is made of plastic and came with an activities kit called "Tricky Pix" that taught kids about trick photography. It has a simple lens, one-click operation, but no flash. The Klutz logo sits above the lens.

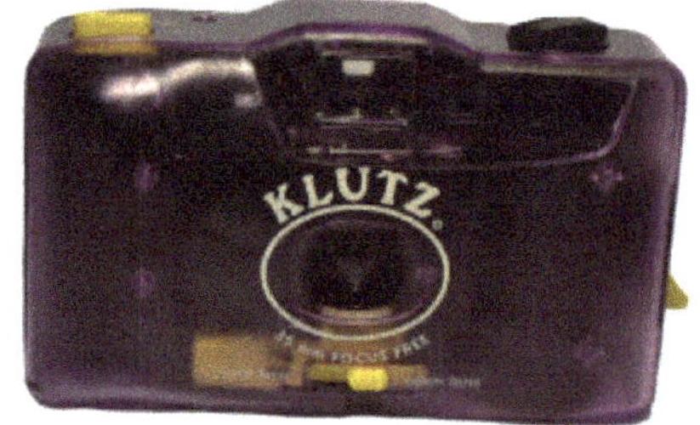

Klutz Press is a publishing company started in 1977 by three friends from Stanford University. Many of their books are spiral bound and teach various crafts. The items needed to complete the tasks are usually included with the book. The Klutz credo: "Create wonderful things, be good, have fun." Camera is reusable and made in China.

$1-$10, camera only; $5-$15, in original packaging

Klutz Press was acquired by Scholastic Inc. in 2002.

Kodak 101 Dalmatians Camera (1997-99)

This 110 cartridge camera (similar to some of the Star 35mm models) has a built-in electronic flash and sliding lens cover and was introduced after the release of the Disney movie in 1996. The front is covered with Dalmatians and the kit came with film, camera, batteries, strap, photo frame, and coupons. In some areas this model was offered at a reduced price as an incentive to trade-in disc cameras. Lens is a 22mm with apertures of f/7 (for daylight) or f/11 (for flash) and the shutter is 1/125th of a second. Licensed by The Walt Disney Corporation and made in China.

$10-$25

Kodak Black & White Camera (2002)

This camera is rather compact in size and is a single-use camera. It comes preloaded with 27 exposures, ISO 400, Kodak black & white roll film; has a Ektanar lens; optical viewfinder; and electronic flash (includes battery). The camera is made in Hungary by/for Eastman Kodak Company, Rochester, NY, USA.

$8-$15

Kodak Fling 110/35mm Cameras (1987-89)

This is Kodak's first entry into the disposable camera market in response to Fuji marketing their single-use camera the Quick-Snap first, only the year before in 1986. The Fling ("the camera and film all in one") was available in either 35mm or 110 models. In 1989 Kodak re-branded their Fling camera and it became the Kodak Fun Saver and has been making them ever since, although they are only available in the 35mm format, today. Some simply have the Kodak name, while others have logos, cartoon characters, or other special designs/designations.

The 110 camera came outfitted with an f/8 lens and 1/120th sec. shutter and preloaded with 24 exposures, ISO 200, Kodak Gold 110 cartridge films. No flash. The original list price was $6.95 for either model and manufactured in Taiwan for Kodak. The 35mm version, the Fling 35, comes preloaded with 24 exposures, ISO 400, Kodak Gold 35mm roll film; both have optical viewfinders and no flash.

$5-$20

Kodak Galactic Camera Kit (1989)

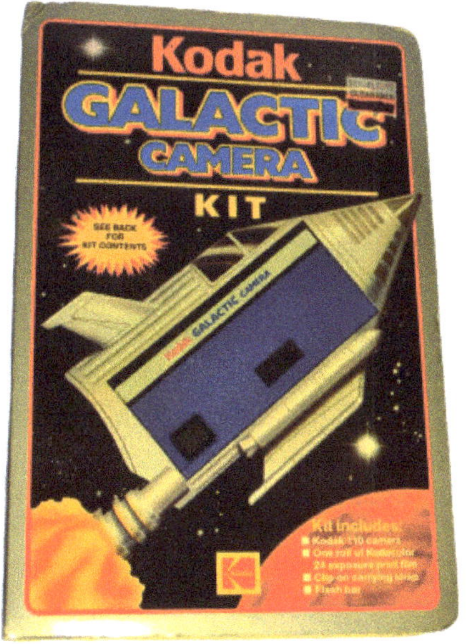

This camera is the same design as the Mickey-Matic 110 camera of 1988. Kit comes complete with camera, 24 exposures, 110 Kodacolor print film cartridge, clip-on carry strap, and a flip-flash bar for flash exposures. There are not very many examples of this camera as it is reported to have been produced in very limited quantities for sales purposes, but never actually went into full production. There is no information about how many were actually produced, but it's safe to say probably not many. It's also safe to say that the packaging of this camera is what stands out most.

Original price was set around $12.99-$14.99 for the kit. It was made in Mexico for ©Eastman Kodak Co., Inc.; uncommon, perhaps rare, and odd that it was made in Mexico when the usual manufacturers were located in the USA, Japan, Taiwan, Hong Kong, and China at that time.

$15-$30 camera alone; $40-$70 complete kit in original packaging.

Kodak Max Waterproof w/Woody Woodpecker Camera (1999)

This is a waterproof camera that takes pictures under water. The cartoon character Woody Woodpecker is featured on the face along with advertising for both Kodak and Universal Studios and their "Islands of Adventure" themed parks which opened in 1999. It comes preloaded with 24 exposures, ISO 800, Kodak Max 35mm color print film; a simple single-element lens, one-click shutter, and optical viewfinder; no flash. ©Eastman Kodak Co. and Universal Studios, Inc., and made by Kodak.

$10-$20

Konica Black & White Camera (2000)

This one is a black plastic body in a cardboard covering that has the Konica name and logo to left of viewfinder. It's a single-use camera that comes preloaded with battery and 18 exposures, ISO 400, 35mm film; fixed focus lens and one click shutter; electronic flash. The package it comes in states "For Promotional Use Only" and "Not For Resale". The camera was made in China and the film made in Japan by Konica; ©Konica Corp.

$8-$15

Konica has roots dating back to 1873 and manufactured many products in the photographic field such as cameras, films, accessories, film processing chemicals and machines; and more recently things like fax machines and laser printers. However, in 2003 Konica merged with Minolta and became Konica Minolta, Tokyo, Japan. https:// en.wikipedia.org/wiki/Konica

Kool-Aid Mega Mountain Twists Camera (1990s)

This 35mm camera has a yellow and black body and was used to promote the Mega Mountain Twists soft drink mix and the camera was awarded after collecting and mail-in drink mix bags. The camera sports a Kineticolor focus-free 28mm, f/11 panoramic lens, with a shutter that operates at 1/125th of a second, but no flash. It was made in China.

$2-$12

Kool-Aid Multi-Color Camera (1990s)

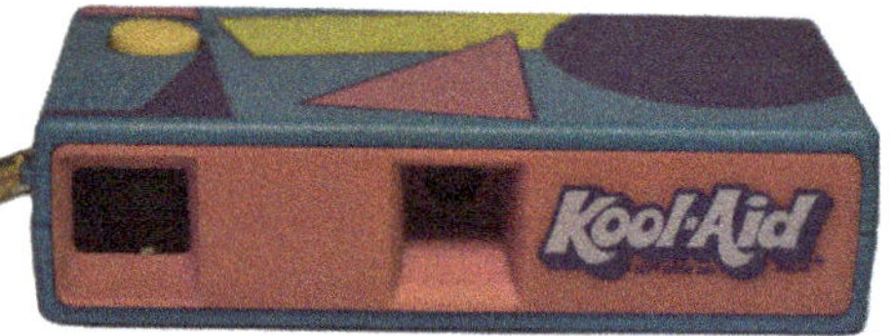

This is a trim-line style camera similar to the Yankees model (see below) and has multi color design. It was used to promote the Kool Aid line of powdered soft drink mix. It uses 110 cartridge films and has no flash. It was made in China. This camera is common.

$2-$12

Kool Aid NY Yankees MicroCam (1986)

Game day giveaway at a New York Yankees baseball game this is a trim-line style camera that uses 110 cartridge films but no flash. It has a sticker on the top and front of the camera that reads "Yankees" and another on the top reads "Kool-Aid." It was made in Taiwan and is somewhat common.

$15-$30

Kraft Cheesasaurus Rex Super Sleuth Camera (1988)

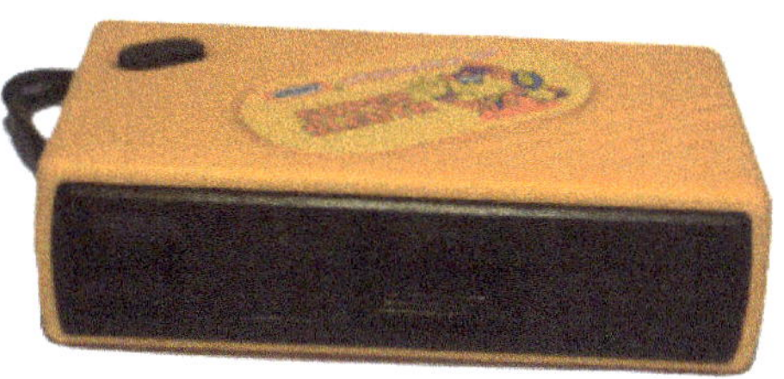

Virtually the same camera design as the Velveeta Shells and Cheese Dinner camera except it has both a black faceplate and matching rear-plate. It was used as a giveaway promotion by Kraft Foods, Inc. On top of the camera is a smaller picture of a cartoon character with a magnifying glass in hand. It features a simple one-click shutter and focus-free lens. It was made in China under license for Kraft Foods Corp., and is fairly common.

$2-$12, camera only; $15-$25 in original packaging

Kraft Velveeta Shells and Cheese Dinner Camera (1988)

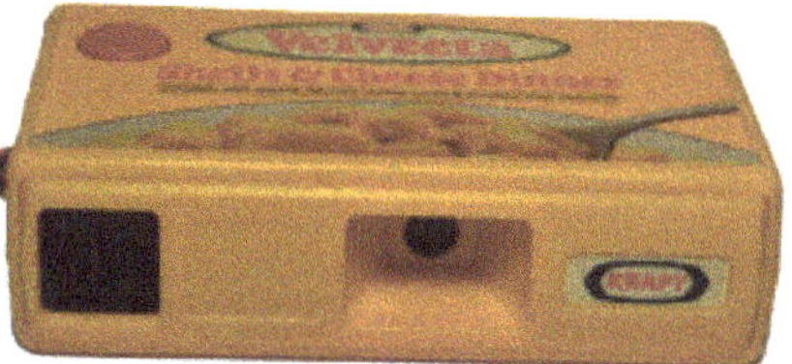

This is a basic product type 110 camera that was used as a giveaway promotion by Kraft Foods, Inc. It has a bright yellow body with "Velveeta Shells & Cheese Dinner" and a photo on the top. It has a simple one-click shutter and focus-free plastic lens. It was made in China under license for Kraft Foods Corp., and is fairly common.

$2-$12, camera only; $15-$25 in original packaging

Land-O-Lakes Camera (1990s)

A cheap 35mm camera given away as a premium by Land-O-Lakes Corp., who have made products like cheese, butter, cream, dips, and other related dairy items since 1921. The camera body is of the generic plastic black-box type with a cardboard covering done in the colors of red on top and bottom, blue on each side, and white on front and back. It has "Say Cheese!" in yellow along with Land-O-Lakes and other printing on the front. It was made in China.

$1-$10

Le Box Camera by Agfa (2002)

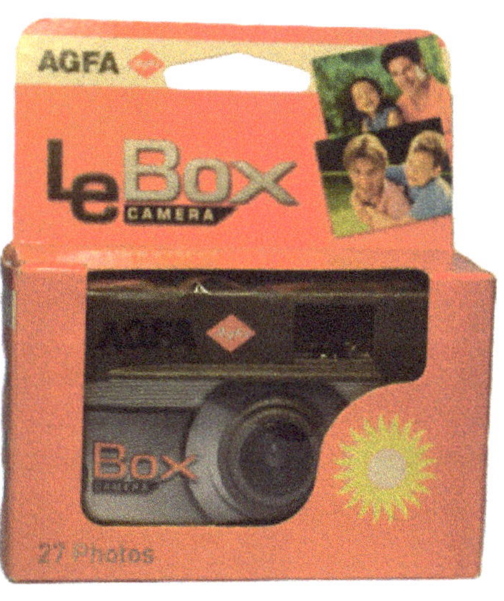

This small single-use plastic camera boasted "Eye Vision Technology" on the box package (no other explanation was given). This camera is compact and grey in color with the Agfa name and logo printed beside the optical viewfinder. It comes preloaded with 27 exposures Agfa Vista 400, 35mm color print film; simple shutter and fixed focus lens; no flash (however, there are flash models along with various colors). The camera body is made in the Czech Republic; and the film and lens is made in Germany by Agfa-Gevaert AG.

$10-$20

Le Box Ocean Camera by Agfa (2005)

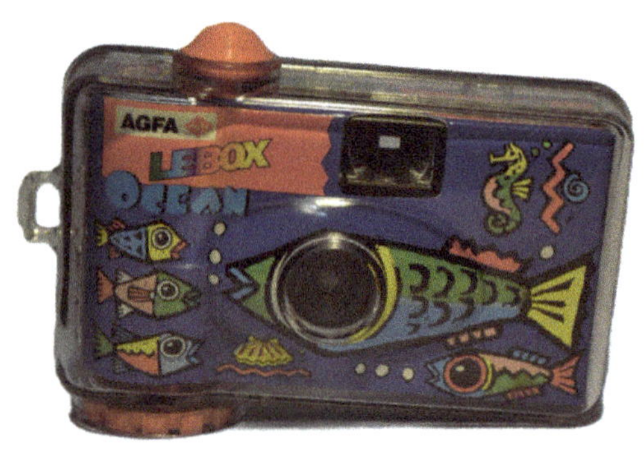

This is a plastic bodied single-use camera with a cardboard covering all contained within a plastic cover so that you can take the camera under water and take pictures. The face of this model is blue with fish depicted on it. It comes preloaded with 27 exposures Agfacolor Vista 400, 35mm color print film; fixed focus lens; simple one click shutter; optical viewfinder; no flash.

The camera was made in China; the film in Germany; ©Agfa-Gevaert AG

$8-$15

Le Clic Cameras (1980s-2000s)

These cameras were available in a variety of colors and color combinations. They come packaged with and without film and batteries. Some use 110 cartridge films, others use 35mm, and still others have APS (advanced photo system). They even made cameras that use "disc film." There is even a translucent camera and a Mini/Micro camera called Le Mini. Le Clic is a brand of Concord Camera.It was made in China.

Le Clic 35mm - $10-$20 camera only; $25-$50 in original packaging

Le Clic Disc - $2-$10 camera only; $12-$20 in original packaging

Le Clic 110 - $5-$15 camera only; $20-$40 in original packaging

Le Clic Translucent LC17 TC, 35mm, with flash - $15-$30

Le Mini by Le Clic - $15-$30 camera only; $25-$45 in original packaging

At one time, Concord Camera was the largest producer of single-use (disposable) cameras as well as more conventional cameras such as 110 cartridge, 35mm or APS. They marketed their cameras under names like Concord, Le Clic, Argus, and Keystone. They also made cameras for corporate customers as incentive give-aways and logo branding. All made in China. Concord Camera ceased operations in 2008.

Lion King 110 Camera (1994)

This camera is a Special Edition 110 camera by Kodak and made for the Walt Disney Corp. as advertisement for their Lion King animated movie that appeared in theaters in 1994. Like the Aladdin animated movie in 1992, Disney's The Lion King grossed over $760 million to make it the highest grossing movie to that date.

The kit also comes with a 110 film cartridge containing 24 exposures, ISO 200, Kodak Gold color print film. It sports a 28mm, f/8 focus free lens and 1/125 sec. mechanical shutter and electronic flash. The front of camera features a small picture of the lion cub Simba beside the lens. It was made in the USA by Eastman Kodak Company and ©Walt Disney Productions, Inc.; uncommon.

$20-$40 camera alone; $90-$120 in unopened original packaging

More about the Lion King animated movie here: https://en.wikipedia.org/wiki/The_Lion_King

Lisa Jane Camera Outfit (2005)

This outfit comes with a reusable plastic camera, 35mm color film, a photo book for your pictures, and is best suited for outdoor use. The face of the camera has a vinyl white sticker with stars printed on it. Another smaller sticker beside the view-finder has the signature of Lisa Jane on it.

The only example found is a purple/lavender colored one so there may be other colors. There are also examples of the Lisa Jane signature on puzzle game boxes and dolls.

The camera offers a focus-free lens and one-click shutter, with no built-in flash, but there is a hot shoe for adding one. It was copyrighted by Lisa Jane/Haley Media, licensed by MGL, UK. It is uncommon.

$5-$15, camera only; $15-$30 in original packaging

As the story goes, Lisa Jane was given a camera by her grandfather at the age of 10. She became fascinated with photography and went on to earn a teaching degree in photography along with a minor in art. She has been honored and awarded for her unique and creative style of photography over the years. Her work shows up in a variety of media including books, posters, greeting cards, calendars, stationary, and fairy dolls. Her photography studio (Eden Studio) is located in Houston, TX, USA. https://bit.ly/lisajaneinfo

Little Tikes 35mm Camera with Flash and Film (1990s)

Made specifically for kids this is a real 35mm focus-free camera for ages five and up. It is a basic point and shoot with built-in flash and the kit included a roll of 12-exposure, ISO 200, 35mm "Little Tykes film." Comes with a carry strap and requires one AAA battery to power the flash. It was made in China.

$1-$10, camera only; $15-$25 in original packaging

Little Tykes 35mm Flash Camera (2004)

Now here is an odd shaped camera- It's rather large for a child's camera and oval in shape. The colors range from blue to red to yellow and green; various colors were available. It uses ISO 200, 35mm roll films; and requires one type AAA battery to power the electronic flash; fixed focus lens; simple shutter; optical viewfinder. It was designed and licensed by Kids Station Toys International, LTD, Miami FL, USA; and made in China; ©The Little Tikes Company, Hudson, Ohio, USA.

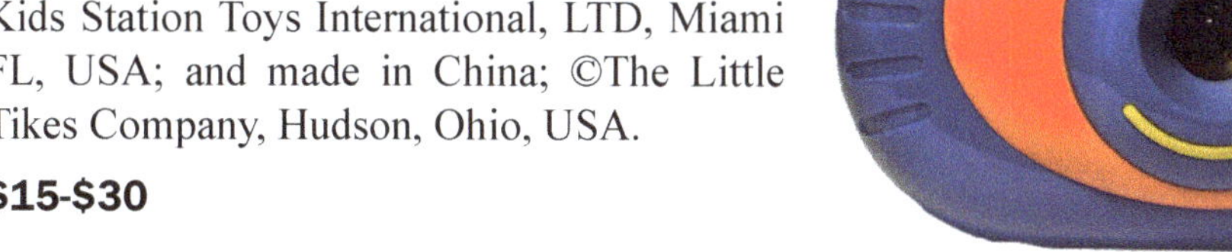

$15-$30

Lo-Fi Orange Juice Box Camera, Lemonade Box Camera, and Fresh Milk Box Camera (2011)

These crazy cameras feature "Lo-Fi output" and "cool color bleeds" along with "vignetted photos" due to the 28mm wide angle plastic lens and each one is in the shape of a juice box with a straw. The straw is actually the shutter release. A very simple 1/100th second shutter speed paired with a 28mm f/9.5 focus free lens; no flash. Any 35mm roll film can be used but ISO 800 is recommended for best results. No batteries required. ©Hype a part of the DLG Group, LTD., UK; and made in China; several other brands and names to watch for; many in the Japanese markets.

$30-$70 camera alone; $70-$150 camera in original blister packaging

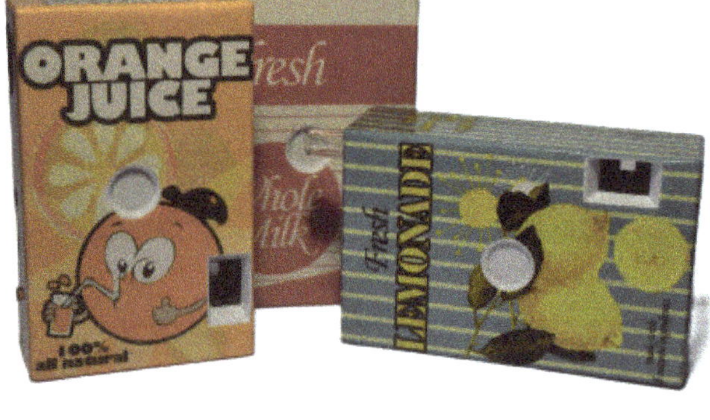

Looney Tunes Outdoor Photo Outfit (1998)

This one uses easy to load 110 cartridge film coupled with simple point and shoot features. The outfit came with a camera, Looney Tunes 110 film, photo album, and stickers. The original list price was $15.00. It was manufactured in China under license by Kalimar,[1] Inc., St. Louis, MO, USA, for Warner Brothers.

$5-$15, camera only; $25-$50, in original packaging

Kalimar was acquired by Tiffen Corp. of Hauppauge, NY, USA, in 1999

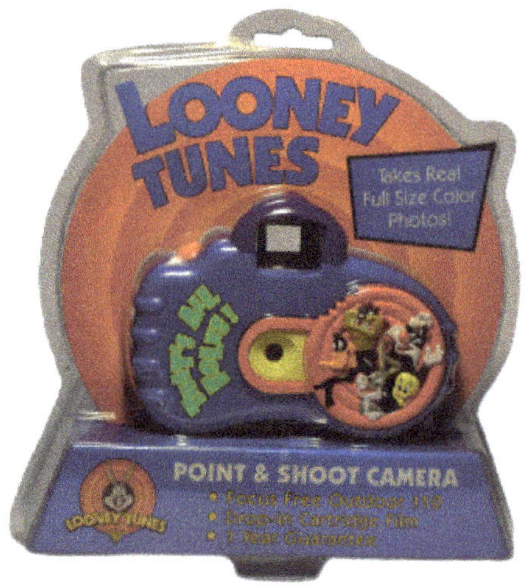

Lucky Strike Disposable Camera (1990s)

This is a simple to use disposable camera used as a promotion for the Lucky Strike brand of cigarettes and has the Lucky Strike logo on face. It has a plastic single-element lens, one-click shutter, and comes preloaded with 27 exposures, ISO 400; 35mm color print film. It has an optical viewfinder; no flash. ©R.J. Reynolds Tobacco Company and made in China. It is uncommon.

$15-$30

Lucky Strike Spy Camera (1950)

According to the only history available, the Lucky Strike camera was created specifically for the U.S. Signal Corps and only two were actually ever made. One can be found at the U.S. Army Signal Corps museum in Fort Gordon, GA, USA, the other has been sold a few times over the years, according to sources. The actual and original name was "Concealable Still Camera."

The camera was made to fit the wrapper of a pack of Lucky Strike Cigarettes (hence the name). It uses 16mm roll-films (good for 18 exposures) and sports a 17.5mm, f/2.7, Zeiss Sonnar lens. The shutter is a four-speed focal plane[3] type. The "cigarettes" sticking up in the pack are the controls for the camera. Came with instructions and a light-meter disguised as a pack of matches. Last known auction sale was in 1991 for around $30,000 at Christies. Obviously it is super rare.

$30,000+

The British American Tobacco Group owns the Lucky Strike brand of cigarettes.

The Zeiss Sonnar lens was highly desirable because of its simple design, quick aperture, and relatively lightweight making it perfect for this application. Dr. Ludwig Bertele designed the lens in 1929, and later, was patented and manufactured by Zeiss Ikon a well known German maker of cameras and lenses. More here: https://bit.ly/ZeissIkon

Focal Plane shutters have the advantage of higher speeds over leaf shutters (ones built-in to the lens). They also have the advantage of being lower cost and the camera here could have had a shutter made of either light metal or fabric sheets. Today, a camera with this shutter design would have lightweight metal or polymer blades allowing flash sync speeds of up to 1/250 sec.

M&M's 110 Cartridge Camera by Le Clic (1980s)

This M&Ms 110 cartridge camera has a built-in electronic flash and was made by the Keystone Camera Company. Camera body is yellow, red, and green with the word "Smile" and four M&M's candy characters on center top along with a M&M's candy bag logo. "Le Clic" is on the face of the camera body. It came with a soft printed carry bag, strap, and instructions. Requires two AA batteries to operate flash. Made for Mars Candy Company as a promotional tool for their M&M's candy line. Licensed by Keystone Camera Company and manufactured by Le Clic in the USA.

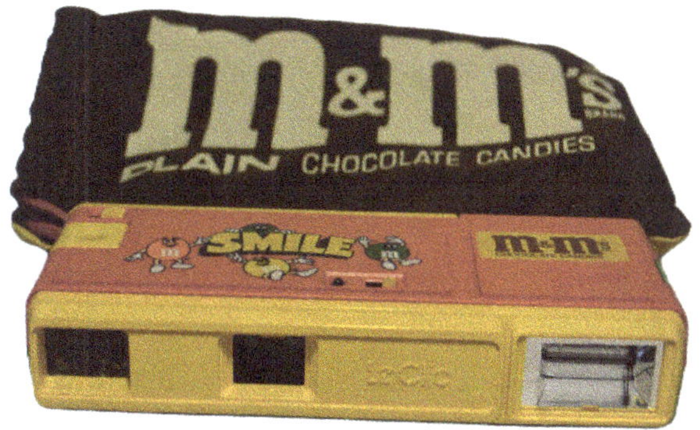

$25-$40

The Keystone Camera Company was an American manufacturer of consumer photographic equipment. The company filed for chapter 11 bankruptcy protection in January 1991. Le Clic was a camera brand made by Keystone Camera. Concord Camera, Inc., continued to use the names Keystone and Le Clic (among others) into the early 21st century.

M&M's 35mm Camera (2001)

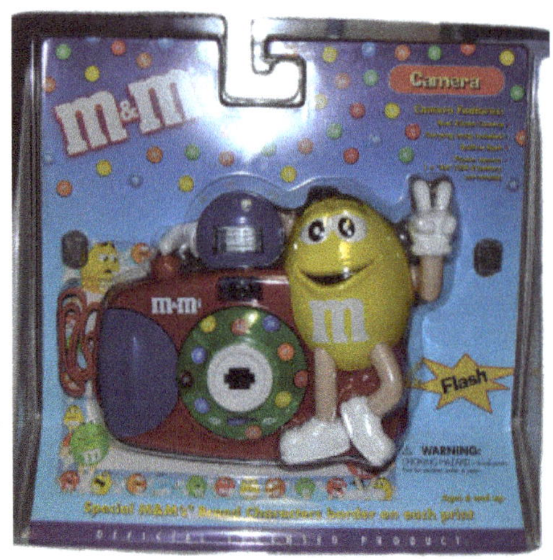

This is a higher than usual quality 35mm camera featuring a large M&M's character as part of the camera with his right hand used as the shutter release. There also are M&M's candies all around the lens and the M&M's logo near the viewfinder. The camera prints a special M&M's brand character border on each print. Comes equipped with a built-in electronic flash (requires one AA battery) and a carry strap with "M&M's" printed on it. This is a M&M's official licensed product (a division of Mars, Inc.) and manufactured and distributed under license by Polyconcept USA, Inc., Stamford, CT, USA. It was made in China.

$20-$30, camera only; $40-$90 in original packaging

M&M Translucent Flash Camera (2003)

This is a 35mm camera with a translucent plastic body camera with the M&M characters shown on the face. Simple one-click shutter and focus-free 35mm, f/11 optical lens with electronic flash. Comes in various colors. Copyrighted (2003) by Masterfoods Corp., it was made in China.

$20-$30

Macy's with Kermit Frog Outdoor Camera (2002)

A plastic red and yellow camera with "Macy's" printed on one side of the front of the camera and Kermit Frog around the lens giving a big "Hi-Ho!" It uses 35mm roll-films and ISO 400 speed is recommended, and it has no flash. It is somewhat common. Copyrighted by Macy's, Inc., it was made in China.

$12-$25

Macy's Thanksgiving Day Parade Camera (2000s)

This single-use camera was a promo for their Thanksgiving Day Parade which they have famously been a part of for decades. It comes preloaded with 24-exposure, ISO 400, 35mm film. Copyrighted by Macy's, Inc., it was made in China.

$12-$25

Mario Andretti-Nigel Mansell Kodak FunSaver Camera (1995)

This is a Kodak FunSaver 35mm disposable camera that has a flash so can be used indoors or outdoors. Comes preloaded with a 24-exposure roll of Kodak color-print film with a "pre-exposed" photo of "Team of Champions," Nigel Mansell (F1) and Mario Andretti (Indy) so there are 23 exposures left to use. Licensed by Kodak and made in the United States.

$20-$30

the MARLBORO section

<u>Marlboro Cigarette Cameras:</u>

There are at least six of these cameras ranging from disposable to reusable and even a spy version. All have one thing in common and that is they promoted the Marlboro name to increase cigarette sales. Another incentive offered was photos taken with the cameras could be sent into Marlboro to win prizes like camera gear, camcorders, and even vacations.

<u>Marlboro Camera – Japan Version (1997)</u>

This reusable plastic model was made in Tokyo, Japan. "Lens made in Japan" is printed under the lens on the face of the camera. It has a f/5.6, 34mm glass lens with flash and uses 35mm roll films. It is uncommon.

$160 asking price found on Ebay. (No picture available.)

<u>Marlboro Disposable Camera (1996)</u>

This disposable camera was produced between 1995 and 1997 and came packed in a plastic wrapping and has a cardboard covering depicting the Marlboro name, colors, and logo. This camera was free if you purchased five packs of cigarettes. It has a cheap plastic lens and comes preloaded with 27-exposure, 35mm color film. No flash. This camera was made by Vivitar Corp. probably in China. Vivitar went out of business in 2008.

$5-$15

<u>Marlboro Radio Camera (1999)</u>

This model allowed you to tune in your favorite radio station and take pictures at the same time. Both AM and FM stations could be tuned in. It requires two AAA batteries to operate and has no flash. Likely made in China. It is rare.

$100+/-

A picture is found here: https://bit.ly/MarlboroCameraRadio

<u>Marlboro Spy Camera (1989)</u>

Spy camera that used Type 110 cartridge films. This one looks like a Marlboro cigarette pack but takes pictures. It was made in the USA. It is uncommon.

$40-$80

<u>Marlboro Sure-Shot by Canon (2000)</u>

<u>Marlboro Sure-Shot Owl by Canon (2000)</u>

These last two Marlboro cameras are made in China by Canon and are both called Sure-Shot: one is simply called the Marlboro Sure-Shot while the other is called the Sure-Shot Owl. Both cameras use 35mm films and have a f/1:4.5 Auto-Focus (AF) lens. The Owl version came in black or silver/gray and both are reusable, with ISO 400 film speed recommended. Exact dates of manufacturing are unknown, but 1997-2001 would seem reasonable.

$20-$40 (either model)

Mars 35mm Camera (1990s)

This is a reusable 35mm focus-free lens camera with built-in flash. This was a promotional camera offered by the Mars Candy Company makers of Mars Bars and M&Ms candies. It is a basic camera with a black body camera and the "Mars" logo on its face. Requires one AA battery to power flash. It was made in China. It is difficult to find but not impossible.

$10-$20

Mars began in 1911 as the Mar-O-Bar Co., a snack food business founded by Frank C. Mars of Tacoma, Washington and now known as Mars, Incorporated of McLean, VA.

Mars Wide Pic Camera (1980s)

An all red plastic 35mm camera that takes panoramic photos. It uses a simple shutter and focus-free lens. Copyrighted by Mars, Inc., it was made in China.

$20-$40

the McDonalds section

McDonald's 101 Dalmatians Camera (1997)

A plastic reusable camera with the design of a Dalmatian dog's spotted fur. It has Disney's 101 Dalmatians printed on the face. There are a couple different designs to watch for. This was a promotional camera for Disney's 101 Dalmatians movie as well as to get people to buy McDonald's foods. Camera uses 35mm roll films and has an electronic flash for indoor shooting. Copyrighted by McDonald's Corp, Inc., and Disney, Inc., it was made in China.

$12-$20 camera only; $25-$50 in original packaging

McDonald's Action Quad Cam (2000s)

This quad-cam snaps four pictures all at once, in four different colors, to create a single print. The iconic McDonald's arches logo is on the face of the camera. It uses any standard 35mm roll-film and has no flash. Copyrighted by McDonald's Corp., Inc. It was made in China.

$2-$12, camera only; $15-$25 in original packaging

McDonald's Bill Elliott Camera (1999)

This one-time use camera is a cheap camera, with a plastic body and a cardboard covering featuring Bill Elliott (NASCAR #94) on the camera face. Comes preloaded with 27-exposure, 35mm color print film and a battery to power the flash. Copyrighted by McDonald's Corp., it was made in China.

$10-$20

McDonald's Burger Camera (1990s)

Cheap plastic body with cardboard covering depicting a delicious McDonald's hamburger and the McDonald's logo with the word "smile" printed on the face. It comes preloaded with standard 35mm color print film and has no flash. Copyrighted by McDonald's Corp., Inc., it was made in China. It is uncommon.

$20-$40

McDonald's Coca-Cola Disposable Camera (1999)

This is a cheap plastic one-time use camera with a red cardboard covering. It has the McDonald's logo with the word "smile" on the upper left of the camera face and the Coca-Cola logo on the lower right side. It comes preloaded with 35mm color print film but has no flash. Copyrighted by McDonald's Corp., Inc., and Coca-Cola, Inc. It was made in China and is somewhat common.

$15-$30

McDonald's European 35mm Camera (1990s)

From the LA PURE collection (the E on PURE is a McDonald's logo turned on its side), this camera is reusable and uses 35mm roll films. The body came in various colors with the McDonald's logo located on the side of the camera body. It has a 35mm focus-free lens and no flash. Copyrighted by McDonald's Corp., Inc., it was made in China and distributed in Europe.

$15-$30

McDonald's Fries Camera (1997)

This is a plastic camera in the shape and colors of a package of McDonald's iconic French fries. The front opens to expose the lens and view-finder. The camera has the McDonald's name and logo on front. The camera uses type 110 cartridge films and there is no flash. Copyrighted by McDonald's Corp., Inc., it was made in China and it is somewhat uncommon.

$80-$100

McDonald's FunShots Camera (1992)

A pocket size camera made by Concord Camera for McDonald's to use as a way to raise money for its "Ronald McDonald Children's Charities of Canada." The camera comes in three colors: green, pink, or orange. The original price was $2.99 and 50 cents of each sale went toward the charity. A 24-exposure 110 film cartridge is also included and there is no flash. Copyrighted by McDonald's Restaurants of Canada, Ltd.

$15-$25

McDonald's Indoor-Outdoor Camera (1998)

This is a basic plastic body with cardboard wrap-around covering. This one depicts the McDonald's colors and arches logo. It comes preloaded with 27-exposure, ISO 400, 35mm, roll-film and a battery to power the flash. Focus-free lens and one-click shutter. Printed on the box is "This camera was recycled, reloaded with quality film, and repackaged by Solo International Corp., Florham, NJ," It is copyrighted by McDonald's Corp.

$15-$30

McDonald's McFoto Disposable Camera (2000)

This single-use indoor/outdoor camera comes preloaded with 27-exposure, ISO 800, 35mm color print film and has an electronic flash. Copyrighted by McDonald's Corp., Inc., it was made in China.

$15-$30

McDonald's Micro 110 (1980s-90s)

This is a plastic keychain mini camera using type 110 cartridge films. It has the Ronald McDonald character printed on the face and "McDonald's" printed on the top of the body and comes in various colors. Copyrighted by McDonald's Corp., it was made in China. It is somewhat uncommon.

$40-$80 (with or without box)

McDonald's Mini 110 Camera (1990s)

Micro 110 camera with an orange front and a green back. It has a sticker depicting the Ronald McDonald character and the McDonald's logo on the upper right of the face. Copyrighted by McDonald's Corp., Inc.

$20-$40

McDonald's Neon Camera (1991)

A reusable plastic camera that has the McDonald's logo displayed on the upper front of the face. It has a focus-free 35mm, f/5.6 lens and uses standard 35mm roll films. No electronic flash but has a hot shoe for one. There are various colors to look for. Copyrighted by McDonald's Corp.

$15-$20, camera only; $25-$50, in original packaging

McDonald's Ronald McDonald Camera (2000s)

A plastic reusable 35mm camera with flash that features Ronald McDonald pictured below flash on camera face. It has a 28mm focus free lens. Copyrighted by McDonald's Corp., Inc. It was made in China.

$20-$40

Michelin Tire 35mm Camera (2003)

A camera with a plastic body with a wrap-around cardboard covering, which is blue with the Michelin logo on the upper face. This is a single-use camera and comes preloaded with 27-exposure, ISO 400, 35mm color film. A built-in battery powered the electronic flash. Copyrighted by Michelin Tire, Inc., it was made in China.

$1-$10

As of September 2008, Michelin became the world's largest tire maker. Michelin manufactures many types of tires including tires for automobiles, motorcycles, bicycles, heavy equipment, and even the space shuttles. Michelin was incorporated in 1889. In 1891 Michelin applied for a patent for a removable pneumatic tire. More here: https://bit.ly/michelin_info

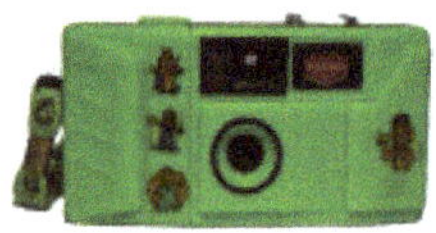

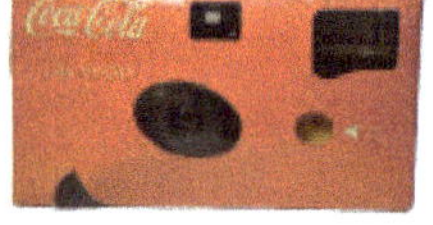

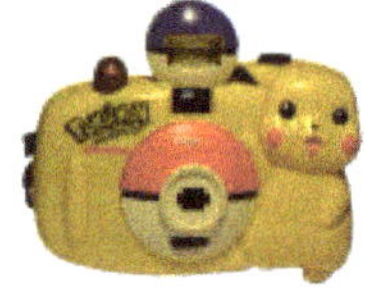

Mickey-Matic 110 Cameras (1989)

The Mickey-Matic is a small hand sized camera that came in two colors: Blue and Pink. There is a sticker picture of Mickey on top of the camera just over the optical viewfinder; another sticker runs along the length of the camera body and states "Mickey-Matic camera by Kodak" on it. This camera used ISO 200, Kodacolor 110 cartridge films; has a 25mm, f/11 lens and 1/90th sec. shutter speed and used a flip-flash bar (no batteries needed) for flash exposures; a carry strap was included. Introduced in 1988 this camera was made over a few years; later, in 1993, it was renamed the Kodak Star 110 and has an electronic flash.

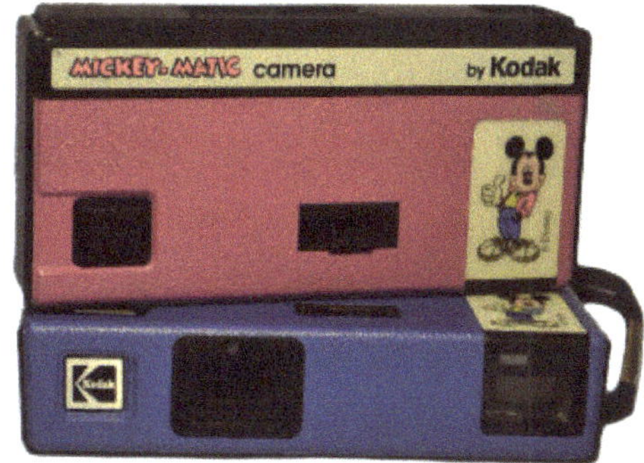

Original price was $12.99 for the kit which included one 24 exposures, 110 cartridge of film. It was made in Mexico for ©Eastman Kodak Co., Inc.; and odd that it was made in Mexico when the usual manufacturers were located in the USA, Japan, Taiwan, Hong Kong, and China at that time. This model is fairly common.

$10-$20 camera alone; $30-$50 in original blister packaging.

Mickey Mouse 127 Camera (1956)

This is a boxy black bakelite camera that uses type 127 roll films (still available). It has a nameplate on face and around lens that has the image of the cartoon character Mickey Mouse along with his name printed beside him. There are also two other locations to find "Mickey"; one is on the film advance knob, and the other is on the back of camera body. According to sources, this camera was only available for sale at Disneyland, CA, USA, and came, in a box, with a flash unit, film, flash bulbs, and carry strap.

It has a simple single element lens and simple mechanical shutter along with a large optical viewfinder and a flash could attach to the side of body via two pins. The camera was made by the Ettelson Corp., Chicago, IL, USA for the ©Walt Disney Company. Uncommon; perhaps rare; and definitely uncommon to have an accompanying original box!

$150-$250 camera alone; $300-$450 if with original box in intact condition.

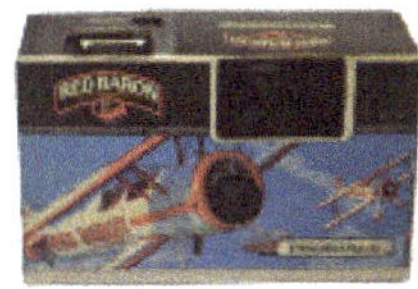

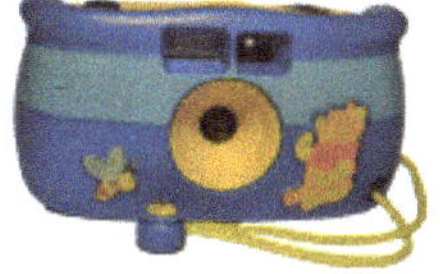

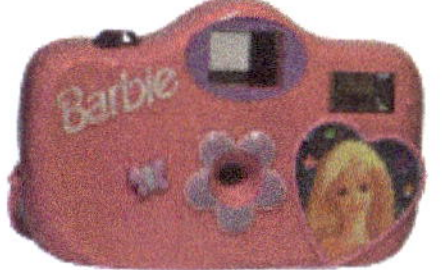

Mickey Mouse 75th Anniversary Camera (2003)

This camera was made to celebrate the 75th Anniversary since Mickey Mouse debuted on film, in 1928, in the first ever sound accompanying cartoon "Steamboat Willie" created and produced by Walt Disney. The camera face features Mickey against a red sun burst background.

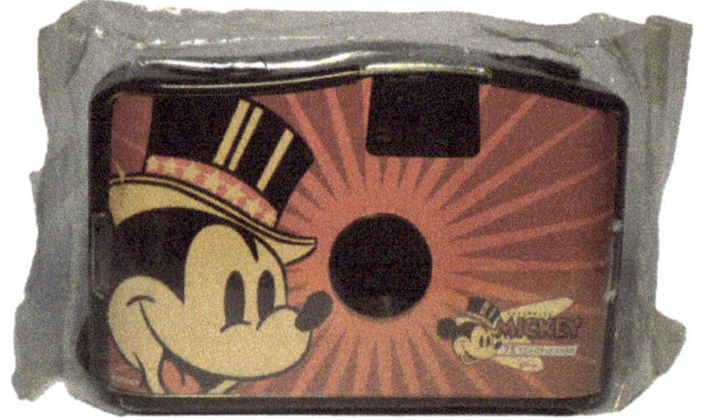

It comes preloaded with 24 exposures, 35mm, ISO 400 Fuji Superia Premium color print film. It also has a 35mm, f/8 lens and 1/100 sec. shutter speed along with an optical viewfinder. No flash. It is made in China by the Fujifilm Corp. for the Walt Disney Company.

$40-$80

More here about the anniversary celebration:
http://www.joshrubinstein.50megs.com/Mickey75/
Main.html#:~:text=November%2018%2C%20
2003%2C%20marked%20the,%22%20on%20November%2018%2C%201928

Mickey Mouse Box Camera (1935)

This is a typical box camera of the era. It's pretty much a cardboard box that is reinforced with wood and is covered with a black "leatherette" material. On the face is a metal plate with the Mickey Mouse character against a red oval. Additionally, the carry strap has "Ensign Mickey Mouse" embossed on it.

Much like the novelty cameras of today it has a simple pre-set lens and one-click shutter operation. Camera used a paper backed roll film called M10 (good for six exposures) that was made in England and has a pull-out wire frame viewfinder for framing your photos. These types of cameras have a film plane measuring 41mm x 31mm; a little larger than a standard 35mm film we still use today. The closest film that equates to M10 is No. 828 roll film which Kodak began making in 1935. It's basically a 35mm roll film without the sprocket holes and has a paper backing.

Originally, this camera was available for purchase alone or as a "Mickey Mouse Photo Outfit" which came outfitted with the camera, darkroom equipment, and developing chemicals. It was made for the Walt Disney Company by Houghton-Ensign Co., London, England. It is uncommon.

$150-$250

Mickey Mouse Brownie Target Six-20 (1946)

This Kodak box camera it seems, by all accounts, has a dubious history attached to it. The story goes as follows: A few of these cameras began showing up at antique dealers in 1995. Previous to this none were known of or available for sale. No one seems able to verify if this is a true Kodak-Disney camera, so it remains a mystery as to whether it's real or fake. Perhaps a prototype for a camera to come but never went into production; a sales tool.

This camera is a Kodak Brownie Target Six-20 model with a Mickey Mouse faceplate; horizontal and vertical waist-level view finders, glass Meniscus lens, and simple one-click shutter w/time exposure setting; used No. 620 roll films. Faceplate reads: Made in USA by Eastman Kodak Company; ©by special permission, Walt Disney Enterprises.

$1500+

Collector's note: No. 620 roll film is the same as No. 120 roll film (still available) except it was rolled onto a special size spool to fit only cameras that use No. 620 film. Therefore, one can re-roll No. 120 film onto a No. 620 spool and then use the film in this camera.

Deeper read: Jim McKeown's Price Guide to Antique & Classic Cameras (2002), page 354.

Historic Camera web site: https://www.historiccamera.com/cgi-bin/librarium2/ pm.cgi?action=app_display&app=datasheet&app_id=2337#google_vignette

Mickey Mouse 126 Camera (1960s)

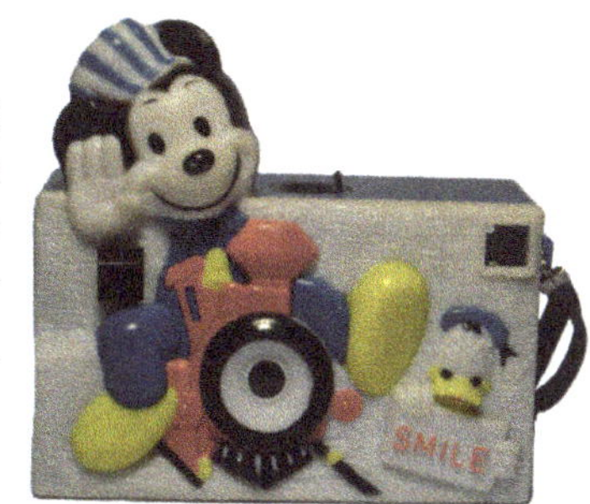

A plastic camera depicting Mickey Mouse in high relief sitting on a train engine that surrounds the lens. Donald Duck is also present on the face, holding a sign that reads "SMILE." It uses 126 film cartridges and Magic-Cubes for flash. Copyrighted by Disney Productions, Inc. It was made in Hong Kong by Helm Toy Corp., and is uncommon.

$35-$55

Mickey Mouse Fun Saver Camera (1994)

This is a point and shoot plastic camera with a cardboard covering depicting a picture of Mickey Mouse, with sunglasses in hand on the beach, along with the Kodak and Disney logos. This is a single-use camera and comes preloaded with 27 exposures, ISO 400, Kodak Gold Ultra 35mm color print film. No flash. It was made in the USA by Eastman Kodak Company; ©Walt Disney Productions, Inc.; and uncommon.

$10-$15 for camera alone; $20-$40 in unopened original box/package.

Interesting Note: The Kodak Fun Saver camera (1989) was originally known as The Kodak Fling camera (1987) which was Kodak's response to Fuji having marketed the first disposable camera, the Quick-Snap, in 1986. It sold for around $10 at the time.

Mickey Mouse Hands Camera (1998)

This camera is made of molded plastic to look as though Mickey Mouse is holding the camera with his hands. However, due to the design, the camera has taken on another reference: The "Butt Hole" Mickey Mouse camera. One can only imagine why; with the camera design looking like he's holding and opening his butt. But I digress, let's move on.

The camera came in a kit and included the camera, a picture frame, one 12 exposures roll of Kodak Max, ISO 400, 35mm color print film and one AA battery to power the electronic flash. It has a single-element focus free lens and simple one-click shutter operation; optical viewfinder. Additionally, the carry strap has a Mickey Mouse head attached at the end. ©Disney and made in China.

$40-$60 camera alone; $80-$120 in original blister packaging.

Mickey Mouse Motor Drive Camera (1995)

This camera has a motor drive film advance so you don't have to advance the film manually. There is a picture of Mickey on face of camera along with a red "M" located under flash. On top of body find "Hi!" and "Mickey Mouse" spelled out. Camera came as a box set containing a camera, roll of ISO 400, 35mm Fujifilm Superia Premium film, and two AA batteries to power the motor and electronic flash. It has a focus free 33mm, f/8 lens and 1/100 sec. shutter speed. It was made in China by Fujifilm Corp. for the Walt Disney Company.

$125-$165

Mickey Mouse (Ompex) Camera (1958)

This camera model is the same as the Kunik brand Ompex 16 except it has the Mickey Mouse and Walt Disney names on the faceplate around lens. The body is dressed in a red leatherette with a chrome top. The interesting thing here is that the camera came with a cardboard full-figure of Mickey solely to display the camera. It is uncommon to find an example with the display, but not impossible.

Additionally, it has a 20mm, f/9 Meniscus lens and 1/50 sec. single-speed shutter and used German made 16mm Tuxi branded roll-films. It was made in Germany for the Kunik Co., Frankfurt, Germany. It's interesting to note here that the Kunik Company was only a distributor of their photographic products and cameras, which were made by different German manufacturers.

This camera had a short run and it is reported that in 1990 perhaps six of these cameras with their Mickey Mouse full-figure displays came to light and were sold for approximately $140 each. That said, it's now 2024 and the camera with or without the display is quite uncommon.

$150-$250 for camera alone; $300-$400 for the camera with display.

Mickey Mouse Red 110 Camera (1980s-90s)

This is an all red colored plastic camera that features Mickey Mouse printed on the face along with "Mickey Wonders Why." On top of camera is design shapes of stars, squares, and triangles. It has a simple single-speed shutter, focus free lens, optical viewfinder, and used type 110 film cartridges. No flash. ©Disney and made in China.

The Mickey Wonders Why is a series of hardcover mail order learning books by Disney where as Mickey asks and wonders about topics like Science, Animals, Our Bodies, The Weather, Dinosaurs, Our Pets, and more; targeted towards younger audiences.

$10-$20

Mickey Mouse XF100 Camera (1960s)

A plastic camera featuring the Mickey Mouse cartoon character on left of face and "©Walt Disney Productions" printed on opposite side. It has a color corrected f/11 lens and 1/50 sec. mechanical shutter coupled with an optical viewfinder. The film type was 126 drop-in cartridges and Magicubes (X cubes) were used for flash pictures. It was made by GAF Corp., Parsippany, NJ, USA, for the Walt Disney Company. GAF stands for General Aniline & Film. Today, GAF is the leading roofing and waterproofing manufacturer in the USA. It is uncommon.

$25-$55

Mickey Mouse Single Use Camera (2006)

This is a plastic bodied camera with a wrap-around cardboard cover depicting Mickey Mouse and Goofy cartoon characters standing in their yard; and is but one of a series of cameras from the "Disney Magic Selections" label. This ready-to-use disposable camera comes preloaded with 27 exposures, ISO 800; 35mm color print film and has an electronic flash. Simple one-click shutter operation, optical viewfinder, and focus free lens. It was distributed by Embassy International, Inc., Cincinnati, OH, USA. ©Walt Disney Productions, Inc. and made in China. It is common and there are other cameras to be found under the Disney Magic Selections label as well.

$15-$30

Micro, Mini or Keychain Novelty Cameras:

These small plastic cameras began showing up in the 1980s as cute little novelties to snap a photo with. The slightly better ones had an actual body into which the 110 film cartridge (available with either 12 or 24 exposures) would be placed. The cheaper ones used the 110 film cartridge as the body of the camera and simply snapped into place. Many were sold with only "Micro 110" or "Mini 110" or even "Baby 110" on faceplate. Many others were sold with no-name.

Many of these micro cameras were fitted with a fixed focus 20mm, f/11 lens and a 1/125 sec. mechanical shutter. None have a flash. There are several body styles and color variations to watch for while collecting these small cameras not to mention the ones with a name-brand or logo on it such as Coca-Cola, Kellogg's Corn Flakes, McDonald's, Simpson's, or one of my favorites, Sesame Street's Muppet Babies.

$1-$5 (for no-name or generic name cameras), $10-$20 (for name or logo cameras.)

Still others will command much higher prices such as the Coca-Cola micro 110 and the Muppet Babies micro which can be valued between **$80-$120 with or without their original box.**

Micro/Mini/Keychain cameras to look for include:

- Cat & Fish
- Cheeseburger
- Chicken & Egg
- Elephant
- Panda
- Fun Gear
- Halina 110
- Le Mini by Le Clic
- McDonald's
- Coca-Cola
- PAIM (French market)
- Sesame Street
- Mickey Mouse/Disney
- Trails End Gourmet Popcorn
- Muppet Babies
- Kellogg's Corn Flakes
- Fun
- Eastern Airlines (Pierre Cardin)
- Girl Talk
- Rockwell
- Donkey Mini 110
- Holga 110* (many colors)
- Dupont Stren
- KFC 110
- Le World
- CitiBank
- Torel
- Ikon 110
- Simpson's Spy
- Kalimar 110
- Hi-Color (Argentina)

- 20th Century Fox
- Hot Shot
- Hot Shot ll
- SupaSnaps
- My First Camera 110 Compact
- Mini Shot
- Superheadz
- Precious Moments
- Taxi
- Big Shot
- Ansco 50
- The Nature Company
- Mini Camera
- The Beverly Hilton
- Film Stars
- Sports Shot
- Mini 110
- Fun Gear
- 007
- Baby 110
- Selby
- Shooter 110
- Lavec Mini Spy
- Vivitar
- Micro Pet
- PF Micro 110
- Gemstar 110
- Spy Cam 110
- Sunpet
- Schwarzenegger (True Lies movie)
- Others…

*The Holga name is also found on 35mm cameras as well.

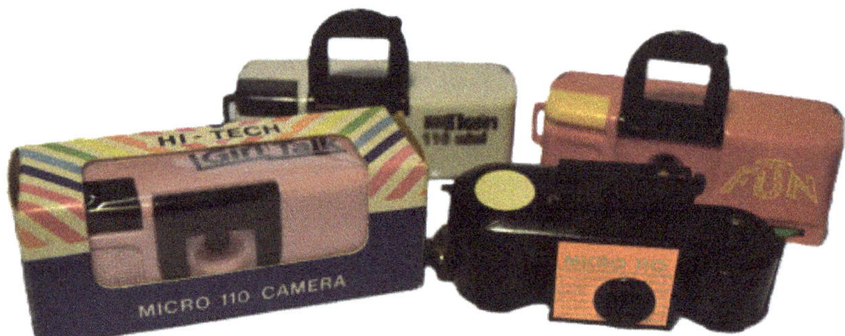

Minolta Weathermatic-A 110 Camera (1980)

This camera floats in water and is good up to 15 feet underwater. It has a built-in flash, which Minolta boasts is the first underwater camera with an electronic flash. It uses 110 cartridge film and it comes with a wrist strap and instructions. There is an optional sports finder and soft pouch case available. Made by the Minolta Corp., New Jersey, USA, and Canada, Ontario.

$15-$30

Mio (the Cow) Camera (1997)

This plastic camera is in the shape of a cow. It was a premium for collecting stickers found on Nestle dairy products. The boxed kit included the camera, instructions to operate, a letter from "Mio" the Cow, and a sticker. Front of the camera has fruits illustrated on it and the peach slides to cover the lens when not in use. It uses standard 35mm films and has a hot shoe for a flash. Shutter speed is 125th of a second and the lens is 35mm, f/8. It was produced for Nestle Dairy Products in Mulgrave, Victoria, Australia.

$30-$50, camera only; $50-$100 in original packaging

Mott's Applesauce 110 "Mil-LOONEY-um" Camera (1999)

This camera was a premium offering from Mott's Applesauce and was co-sponsored by Mott's Applesauce and Warner Bros.' Looney Tunes. They called it the "Mil-LOONEY-um" camera as it was made for the 2000 Millennium. Both the box and camera were printed with Looney Tunes cartoon character favorites: Sylvester and Tweety, Road Runner, Wile E Coyote, Bugs Bunny, Daffy Duck, and Taz. It uses 110 film cartridges and has a simple one-click shutter and focus-free lens. This camera is sought after by camera collectors and Looney Tunes collectors alike. It was manufactured under license by Kalimar, Inc., and made in China. It is a great collectible and commonly found.

$15-$30

Kalimar, Inc. was acquired by Tiffen Corp. of Hauppauge, NY, USA, in 1999.

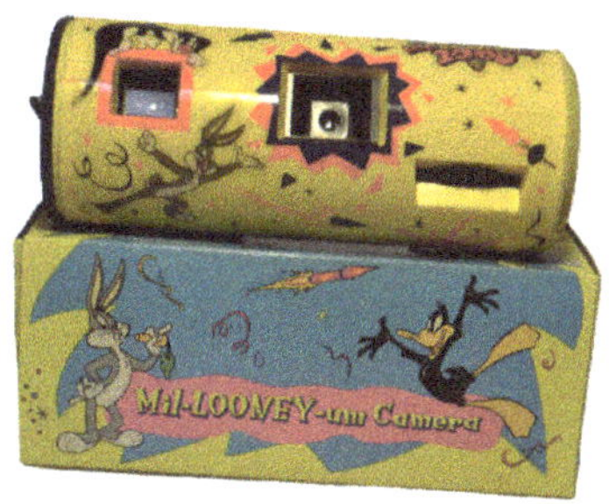
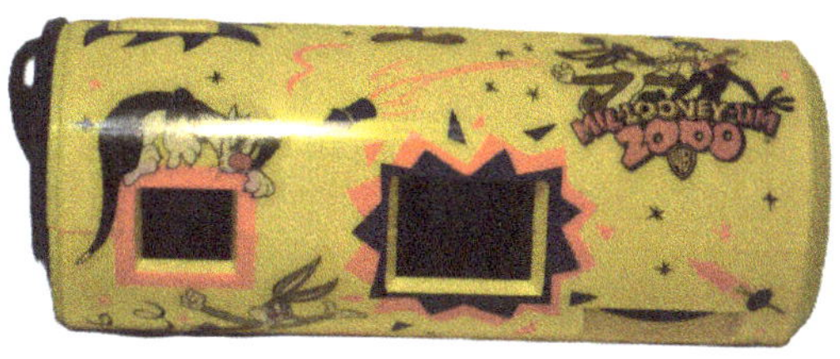

MountaineeR 35mm Camera (1990s)

It's made of plastic and sports the MountaineeR Race Track & Gaming Resort name and logo printed on face. They are located in the northern panhandle of West Virginia, USA. The camera uses standard 35mm roll films; has a focus free 28mm, f/8 optical lens; 1/100th sec. shutter speed; optical viewfinder; no flash. It was made in China and most likely a hand-out promotional item to promote their resort.

$1-$10

https://www.cnty.com/mountaineer/

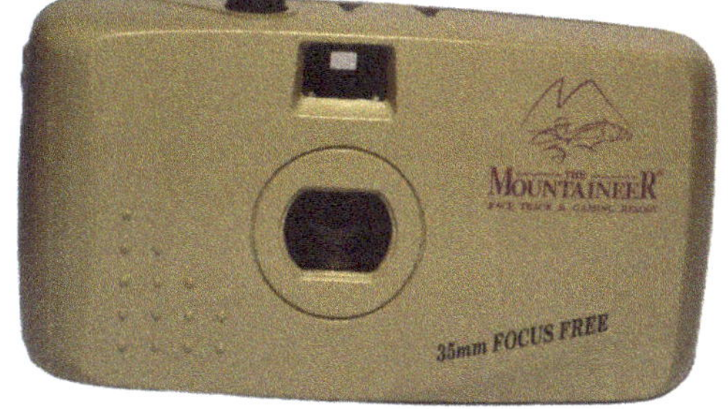

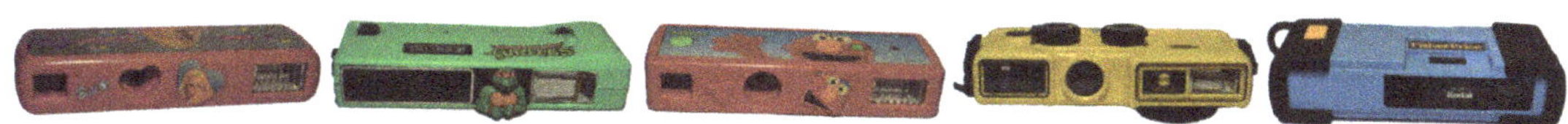

Mudd 35mm Camera (1990s)

A reusable plastic 35mm camera with the Mudd name on the face. The camera was used to promote the Mudd Jeans line of clothing, shoes, and accessories, to young adult women and teens. It has an electronic flash requiring one AA battery to operate. Focus-free 28mm lens and one-click shutter. It uses standard 35mm roll-films. It was made in China.

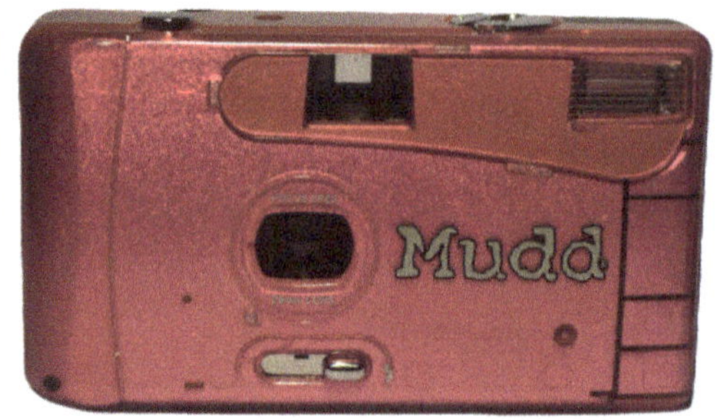

$2-$12

Mudd Jeans was established in 1995. Iconix Brand Group purchased Mudd in 2006. They also own other home and fashion brands. More here: https://bit.ly/muddjeans

Muppet Babies "Magic Box" Micro 110 Camera (1980s)

Small micro 110 camera and keychain. The film canister itself makes up most of the body of the camera, which features a simple one click shutter and fixed-focus f/8 lens. It has "Jim Henson Presents" printed above the Muppet Babies name on the face-sticker. It was made in Taiwan and licensed by The Jim Henson Company, now The Muppets Studio, LLC (formed in 2004), a wholly owned subsidiary of media conglomerate The Walt Disney Company. This camera is sought after by both camera collectors and Sesame Street collectors. If not rare, certainly uncommon.

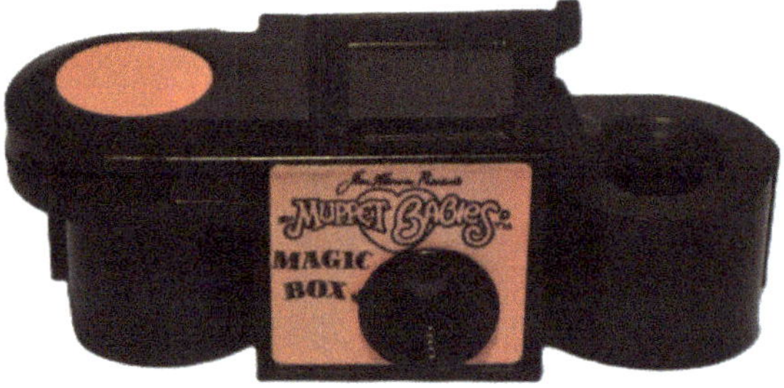

$90-$130

Sesame Street is one of the most highly regard-
ed, and most watched, educational shows for children in the world.

My Crystal LX-22 Japanese 35mm Camera (1993)

This is a see-through clear camera and you can watch all the workings of the camera as you use it. The camera is the same design as the Japanese Bandai made LX-22 and sports a 35mm Ricoh made f/4.5, 3-element fixed focus lens. It also has a 1/125 sec. shutter speed, optical viewfinder, and an electronic flash which requires two AA batteries to operate.

The camera uses 35mm roll films and can be set to one of four ISO settings: 100, 200, 400, or 1000. It even has a self timer! It was made by Ricoh in collaboration with ©Bandai Co., LTD., Tokyo, Japan and made in Taiwan. Bandai is a Japanese toy manufacturer. This camera was released only in Japan and is uncommon.

$200-$450

My First Camera by Sakar (1990s)

This camera sports EZ-Grip handles to make it easier for kids to hold the camera. It also has an extra large optical viewfinder for easier viewing and came in various colors. There are models with an electronic flash and models without a flash. The ones with a flash require two type AA batteries to operate; uses standard 35mm roll films; focus free lens and simple shutter.

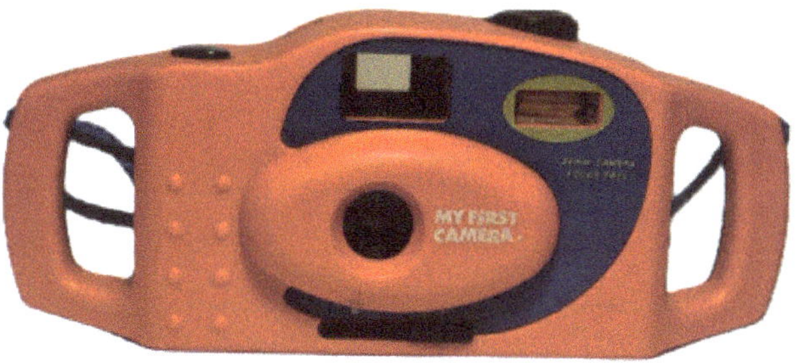

It's made in China for Sakar International, Inc., Edison, NJ, USA.

$10-$30

My Little Pony Friendship Flash Camera (2004)

This is a real reusable 35mm indoor-outdoor camera with a fixed focus 26.7mm, 2 element lens, and preloaded with a roll of 27 exposures, 35mm DX ISO 400 film; optical viewfinder; electronic flash. The combo included 6 Pony Stickers, camera bag, and one type AA battery (for flash). It was made in China and distributed by Sapphire Imaging, LLC, Rochester, NY, USA and licensed by Hasbro Properties Group; ©2004 Hasbro

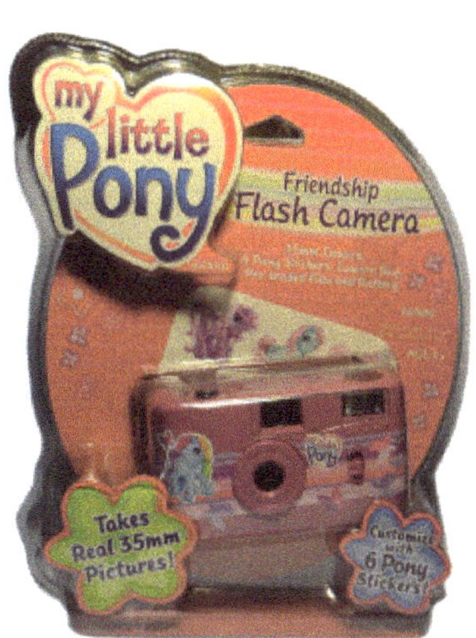

$10-$25

First appearing in 1983, Hasbro offered their line of toy ponies to young girls which in turn were very popular for many years from

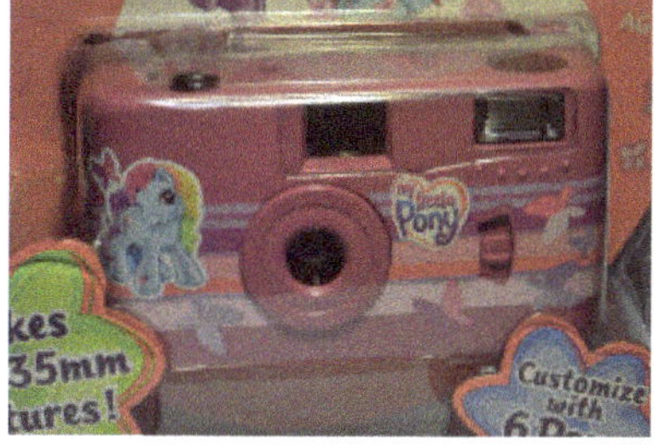

1983 to 1995. A re- launch of the My Little Pony brand took place between 1997-2003. In 2008 My Little Pony celebrated its 25th Anniversary.

Hasbro is known world wide for their toy manufacturing and is mostly owned by the Vangaurd Group.

My Melody Camera by Yashica (2023)

This single-use camera is rather new and features the My Melody rabbit cartoon character holding a ice cream cone with a heart just overhead stating "My best flavor!" printed across it. The camera comes preloaded with 27 exposures, ISO 400, 35mm color print film. It has a fixed focus lens set at f/11; optical viewfinder; 1/125 sec. shutter speed; electronic flash with preloaded type AAA battery to operate. It is/was made in China by Yashica Camera Corp. for 100 Enterprises International Group Co., Ltd. under license of Sanrio Wave HK; ©2023 Sanrio Co., LTD., Tokyo, Japan.

$25-$35

NBC Camera (1990s)

This is a promotional camera to promote the NBC TV Network. It uses standard 35mm roll films and has a 35mm, f.5.6 lens. A CDS sensor sets aperture and shutter speed. It has an electronic flash and requires two AA batteries to operate the camera and flash. The NBC logo including its famous peacock is printed on the face. Copyrighted by NBC, Inc. It was made in China.

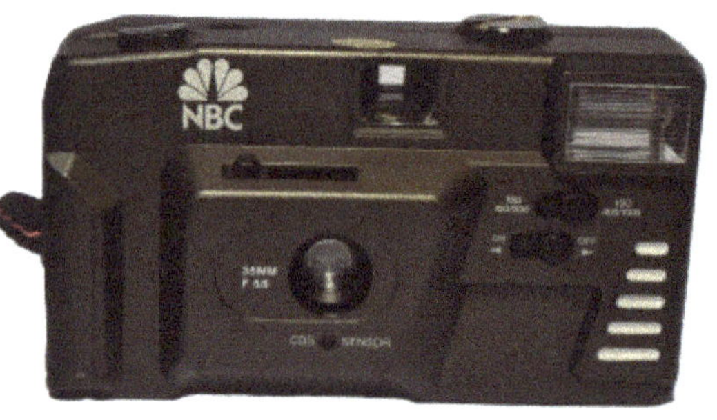

$12-$25

New York & Company 35mm Camera (pre-2020)

This plastic camera is yellow and black in color and sports the NY & Co. name and logo on top of body. It uses standard 35mm roll films; has a simple lens and shutter; optical viewfinder; no flash; made in China. This was probably a promotional give-away. The New York & Company began in 1918 and is a leading specialty manufacturer of women's fashion apparel and accessories and located in New York City, USA. They filed for bank-ruptcy in 2020 and are an on-line, e-commerce only, store now.

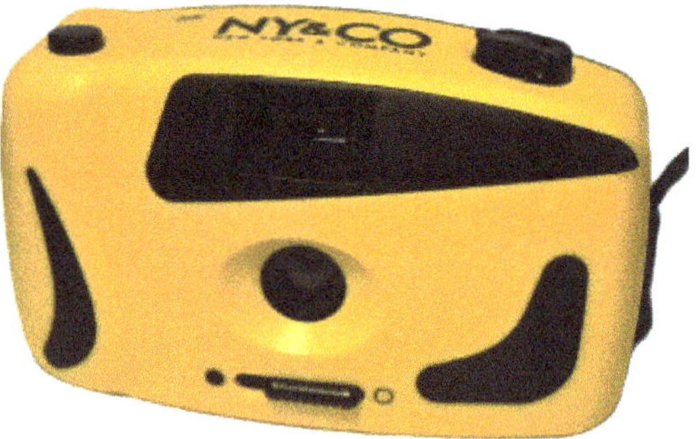

$10-$20

Newport 110 Outdoor Camera (1988)

This camera is virtually the same camera design as the Kraft Velveeta Shells and Cheese Dinner camera and the Kraft Cheesasaurus Rex Super Sleuth camera except this one is all green with the "Newport" logo (orange) on the face of the camera. "Alive With Pleasure Newport," is printed on the top of the camera, also in orange. It uses 110 film cartridges, no flash, simple one-click shutter and focus-free lens. The camera was free with the purchase of two packs of Newport brand cigarettes. Manufactured under license by Kalimar, Inc. It was made in China. It is common but a nice collectible.

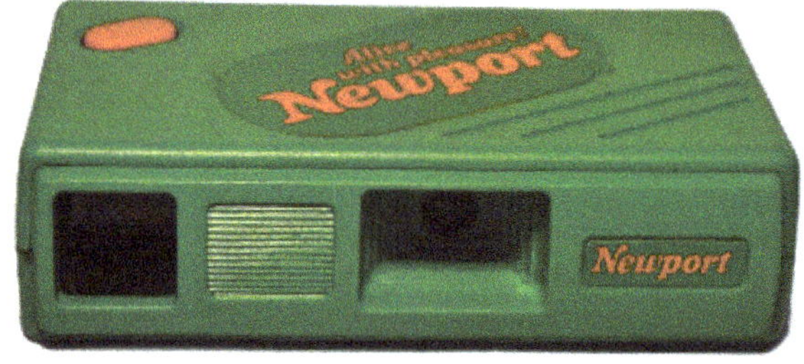

$5-$15, camera only; $15-$30, in original packaging)

Kalimar, Inc. was acquired by Tiffen Corp. of Hauppauge, NY, USA, in 1999.

Nickelodeon Photo Blaster 35mm Camera (1997-99)

(Model N6800)

This is a large colorful plastic camera that has two lenses. Each lens takes its turn exposing the film, so four pictures can be taken on each 35mm frame. It uses 35mm films (ISO 400 recommended); has two fixed focus lenses; simple shutter; optical viewfinder; and electronic flash. Two type AA batteries are required to operate flash. It's made in China by Long Hall Technologies, LLC, of Farmingdale, NY, USA, and the original retail price was $39.95; ©Viacom International, Inc., NY, NY, USA; and while not rare it is uncommon.

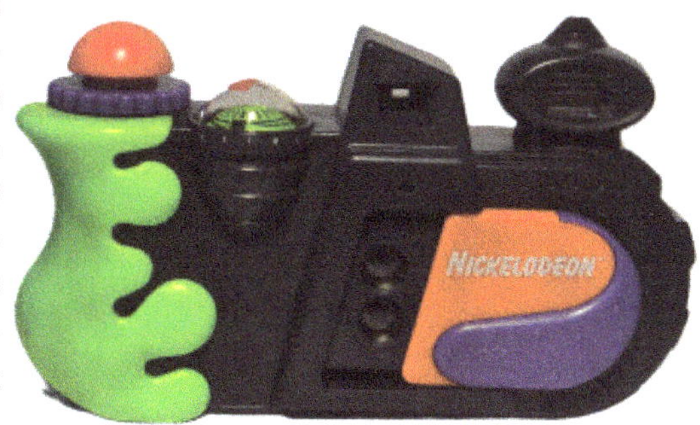

Author note:

Another camera that is the same model design as the Photo Blaster but has a different color scheme is one called Xtreme Pix Go Photo; also uncommon.

$100-$200

Nintendo 64 Compact Camera (1990s)

This rather cheap plastic camera came in various colors and with various other items such as a roll of 35mm Konica brand film, binoculars, or radio. This is a reusable camera, but with no flash, best suited for outdoor photography. It has a simple one-click shutter and focus-free lens. Oddly, this camera has a tripod socket. Copyrighted by Nintendo of America, Inc., it was made in China. It is somewhat common.

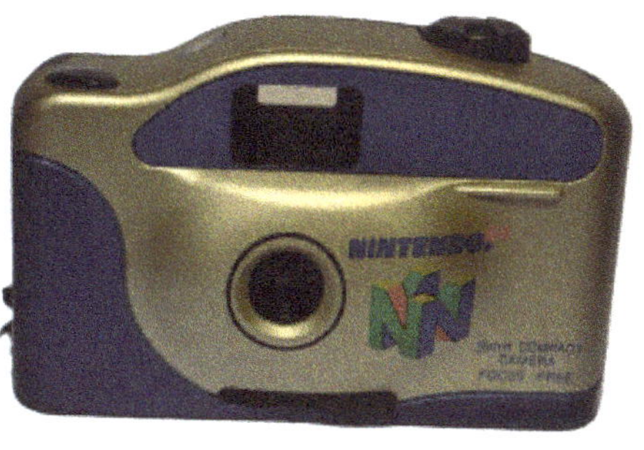

$10-$20, camera only; $80-$120, in original packaging

Nintendo 64 Radio/Camera Set (1998)

This camera set came with a 35mm camera and a AM/FM radio complete with earphones and an arm strap. Two AA batteries are required to operate the radio. Focus-free lens with a 35mm Mega-View viewfinder, no flash and no batteries are needed for the camera. It comes in various colors. Made in China, it is copyrighted by Nintendo of America, Inc.

$10-$20, camera only; $170+/-, in original packaging

Nintendo Super Mario 64 110 Camera (1980s)

This is a plastic trim-line style camera with an electronic flash. It has a simple one-click shutter, focus-free lens and uses 110 cartridge films. The face of the camera has a red front with "Nintendo" logo and a green rear film door. On top of the camera it reads, "Super Mario 64." Requires two AA batteries to operate the flash. Copyrighted by Nintendo of America, Inc., it was made in China.

$15-$30, camera only; $90-$120, in original packaging

Nintendo Super Mario 64 Disposable Camera (1996)

This is a one-time use, point-and-shoot plastic camera with a wrap-around cardboard covering depicting the character Super Mario and "Super Mario 64" printed on the face. Comes preloaded with 24-exposure, 35mm, 400 ASA color print film, has a built-in electronic flash, simple lens, and shutter. It was made in China and copyrighted by Nintendo of America, Inc. It is uncommon.

$15-$30. camera only; $75-$150, in original packaging

Northwest Airlines Single-Use Camera (1993)

This disposable camera has the Northwest Airlines name and logo on face along with picture postcards of different destinations. The camera was a promotional give-away for booking a flight on their airline and comes pre-loaded with 24 exposure, ISO 100, 35mm color print film; has a simple single-element lens and one click shutter: no flash. ©Hachi International, Inc., NY, NY, USA and made in China.

$12-$25

Northwest Airlines began operations in 1926 and was headquartered in Eagan, Minnesota. In 2010 they merged with Delta Air Lines.

Octopus "The Weekender" Camera Radio (1983)

This camera was apparently named the Octopus due to its many functions. It's an alarm clock and a stop-watch, AM-FM transistor radio, has a small storage compartment, along with a flashlight and built-in 110 cartridge film camera (which is an Ansco 600 110 camera) along with an electronic flash. Dubbed "The Weekender" because of its many uses, and originally sold for around $75. It was made in USA by Hendren Enterprise, Harrodsburg, KY, USA. It is reported that approximately 5000 of these were made so they may not be easy to find especially in fine condition; odd but fun collectible; considered rare.

$40-$80

More about the Octopus Weekender here, plus many pictures: https://utahfilmphotography.com/2024/02/14/octopus-the-weekender/

And here: https://kosmofoto.com/2018/08/kosmopedia-octopus-weekender/

Olay Camera by Fuji (2004)

This camera is by the company that produces Oil of Olay products. It is made by Fuji Photo Film, Inc., and is one of their "Quick-Snap" camera products. It has a simple plastic body with a cardboard wrap-around cover that has "Olay" printed on the face along with the logo. It comes preloaded with 15-exposure, ISO 400, 35mm film, and it has a simple shutter and focus-free lens. Assembled in the United States, it is copyrighted by Fuji, Inc.

$2-$12

Old Grand Dad 35mm Camera (1993)

This is a most unassuming camera design. It's made of cheap plastic and all black in color with a red oval line around lens. On the back of camera body is where you will find the Old Grand Dad logo; used to promote their brand of Kentucky whiskey. It has a 25mm, f/8 focus free lens, 1/120 sec. one-click shutter, and optical viewfinder; doesn't have a built-in electronic flash but does have a hot shoe to add one. Any standard 35mm roll films will work in this model. ©Old Grand-Dad Distillery Co., Frankfort, KY, USA; and made in China.

$5-$15 camera alone; $15-30 with original box and instructions

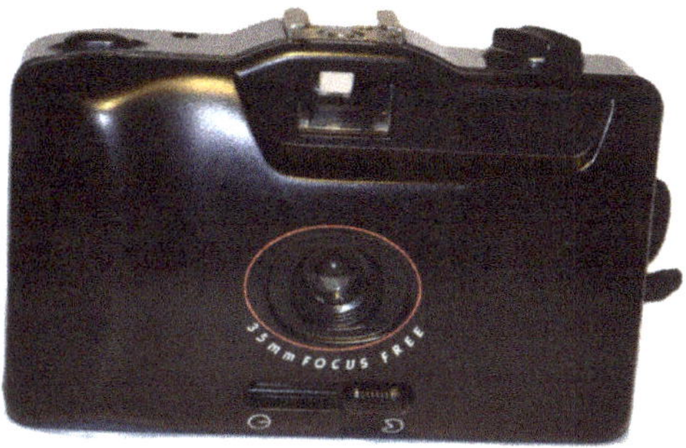

front

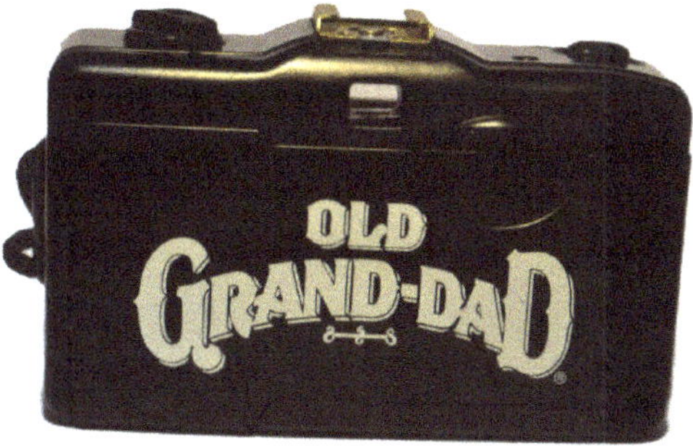

back

Old Grand-Dad bourbon was first made in 1840 by Ray Hayden and named after his grandfather who was highly known for his distilling of alcoholic spirits. The company went through several changes of ownership since those beginning days but Old Grand-Dad ranks in the top ten best selling whiskeys in the USA. Today, Old Grand-Dad bourbon is owned and distilled by the Jim Beam distillery located in Clermont, KY, USA. Suntory Global Spirits, formally Beam Suntory, Inc., bought out Beam in 2014. It's interesting to note here that James Beam started distilling spirits in 1795.

Oreo 35mm Camera (1990s)

A cheap camera with a silver front and black back, it has "Oreo¹" printed on the face beside the lens. It uses 35mm roll-films, has a one speed shutter and focus-free plastic lens but no flash. Copyrighted by Nabisco, Inc., it was made in China.

$5-$15

Nabisco introduced the Oreo cookie in 1912 as competition to the Hydrox cookie on the market just four years earlier in 1908.. Not only are Oreos the best selling cookie here in the United States, but it has become the best selling cookie worldwide. https://bit.ly/OreoCookieInfo

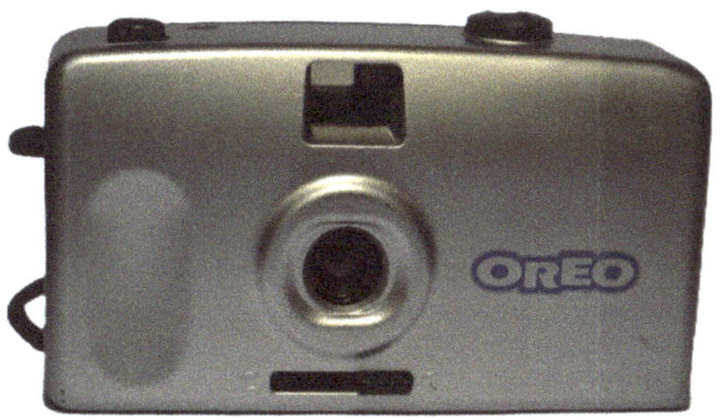

Panaview 35mm Underwater Camera (1990s)

This underwater camera can be removed from its plastic covering to be used on land without the bulky underwater cover. It has an optical viewfinder as well as a pop-up plastic finder on top of cover housing, presumably to use while taking pictures under water. The lens is 25mm and focus free; simple one click shutter; and electronic flash (requires one type AA battery); made in China.

$10-$20

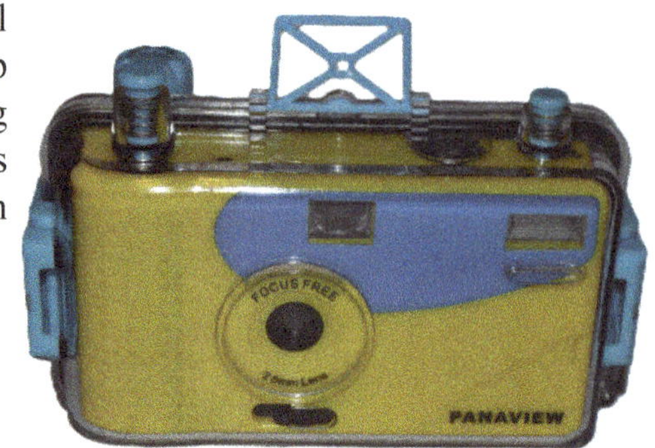

Peko-chan Camera (1990s-2000s)

A plastic reusable 35mm camera depicting the Peko-chan mascot character. One model has a flash shoe for an electronic flash, and another has a built-in electronic flash. All use standard 35mm films and were made in Japan.

$40-$80 (most models)

The Peko-chan character is the mascot (a girl in pigtails licking her lips) of a chain of candy stores and restaurants well known across Japan called Fujiya Co., Ltd. They first opened a shop in Yokohama in 1910 and much later their first "off-shore" store in Taipei, Taiwan, in 2016. *More here: https://bit.ly/FujiyaInfo*

Penny King Feather-Weight Camera (1955)

A plastic camera made by the Penny King Company of Pittsburgh, PA, USA. The camera sported a 55mm, f/11 "Magic lens" and 1/50 second shutter speed and uses type 127 roll-film (still available[2]) to produce 16 exposures. It was made in Hong Kong.

$10-$15, camera only: $15-$30, in original packaging

The Penny King Company began operations in 1949, producing charms for the expanding vending machine market. These charms came with a piece of candy usually costing a penny. They were located in Pittsburgh, PA, USA. In 1955, they became owners and national sales agent for the large vendor machine company Atlas Master, in business since 1930. The machines operated on one cent, a nickel, or a quarter depending upon selection. Presumably, the camera was a promotional tool for the company after their acquisition of Atlas Master.

127 roll-film was introduced by Kodak in 1912 and ran continually until 1995 when Kodak discontinued its manufacture. The good news here is that you can still get the 127 films and get them developed at The Darkroom, San Clemente, CA, USA (since 1976).

https://bit.ly/TheDarkroomPhoto

For a list of currently available photographic films visit here: https://bit.ly/photographicfilms

Peppermayo Waterproof 35mm Camera (2024)

Now here is a rather new entrant into the underwater world of photography. This camera is waterproof to 3 meters depth and is reusable. And get this: it has a removable plastic waterproof casing so you can walk around and take shots but doesn't have to have the bulky waterproof case. The design is described as "super cute retro print design" and features a swirl of blue and white colors along with "Peppermayo" (in yellow) printed just below lens. It has a fixed-focus 28mm lens and uses any standard 35mm roll film (ISO 400 recommended); optical viewfinder; simple one-click shutter and no flash. Peppermayo is a leading fashion brand located in Australia and owned by Georgia Wright. The camera carries the Peppermayo brand name.

$38 +/-

Picture The Millennium Flash Camera by Kodak (2000)

This "limited edition hand-out premium" to Kodak employees was to commemorate the Millennium and build a positive attitude about the future of "pictures" (mostly film). The basic flash camera comes preloaded with a 27-exposure roll of Kodak 35mm film. It also has an employee message printed on the back of the camera package. Licensed by Kodak Corp., and made in China, it is uncommon.

$10-$20, camera only; $40-$60 in original package)

Piggly Wiggly Disposable Camera (1999)

A cheap plastic camera body with cardboard covering depicting the Piggly Wiggly Pig on the front. It comes preloaded with 35mm, 27-exposure, ISO 400 color film and has a built-in electronic flash. Printed and packaged in the United States, it was copyrighted by Piggly Wiggly, LLC.

$2-$12

A man named Clarence Saunders came up with what he thought was a really good idea. During this period in time (early 20th century), it was customary to hand a grocery list to a clerk who would then fill your order. Saunders' idea was to open a self-service shopping experience format. He named his store Piggly Wiggly and opened the doors on September 6, 1916, in Memphis, TN, USA. He is credited for opening the first true self-service grocery store in America. Today Piggly Wiggly has over 500 stores operating in 18 states.
More information here: https://bit.ly/PiggylyWiggly

Pingo 35mm Camera (1986)

This is a simple film camera using 35mm films with no flash. "Pingo the Penguin," wearing a red and white cap, makes up much of the camera body which has "Pingo" printed on face of the camera. Pingo is part of the children's series "Pingu" that ran on Swiss TV from 1986-2000. Copyrighted by IpingVin and made by Nickname. It is uncommon.

$35-$55, with one known sale for $140 in 08-09-21

Pipo Character Camera (1983)

This is a red all-plastic camera depicting the French character "Pipo" holding an ice cream cone in one hand. A little bird is also on the front face. On the back there is a small oval with "pipo" inside. The camera uses 126 cartridge films and Magic Cubes for flash. Made exclusively for the French market in Hong Kong. It is uncommon.

$80+

Planet Hollywood Camera (1997)

A rather uninspiring camera with a black cardboard covering over a black plastic body with "Planet Hollywood" printed on the front. It comes preloaded with 27-exposure, ISO 200, 35mm film, and a battery for the flash. It features a focus-free lens and one-click shutter action. Original price at Planet Hollywood was around $18, but some discount stores sold it for $3.99.

$5-$15

Playboy 40th Anniversary Camera (1994)

This cheap plastic body camera with a cardboard wrap-around depicting Playboy's 40th Anniversary on the face. It comes preloaded with 27-exposure, ISO 400, 35mm color print film. It features a focus-free lens, a built-in flash and simple one-click shutter. It was made in Japan by Fuji Photo Film Co., LTD., Tokyo.

$5-$15, camera only, $15-$30, in original packaging

Playboy 2000 Camera (1998)

This camera was to entice women to compete to become the Playmate of the Year 2000. The winner was to become the January 2000 issue Playmate. In addition, she would receive a "special fee" of $200,000 and represent Playboy throughout the year 2000 celebration. Camera is a rather unassuming plastic one with "Playmate 2000" on its face. Produced by The Edge Sports, USA, under license by Playboy Enterprises, Inc.

$5-$15, camera only; $10-$20 in original packaging

the **POKEMON** section

Pokemon Cameras

Researching Pokemon cameras, only nine were found. Some were available in the United States, while others were made for the Japanese market. A couple models are cheap versions of 35mm cameras to commemorate a Pokemon movie or game. One was a giveaway from a cereal company and another was a hand-out at a convention. The others have strong relief patterns on them and are worth more than the cheapies. Camera collectors are in direct competition with the Pokemon collectors for these items.

Pokemon Cereal Promo Camera (1999)

This blue "pocket cam" has a bright yellow strap with "Pokemon" printed on it and was part of a Cap'n Crunch cereal promotion giveaway. A rather plain cheap plastic camera that uses 35mm films and features a printed Pikachu on its face with the slogan "Gotta Catch 'Em All" printed directly under. No built-in flash but it does have a flash shoe. Manufactured under license for Nintendo by Tiger Electronics, Ltd., USA (parent Hasbro, Inc.), It was made in China.

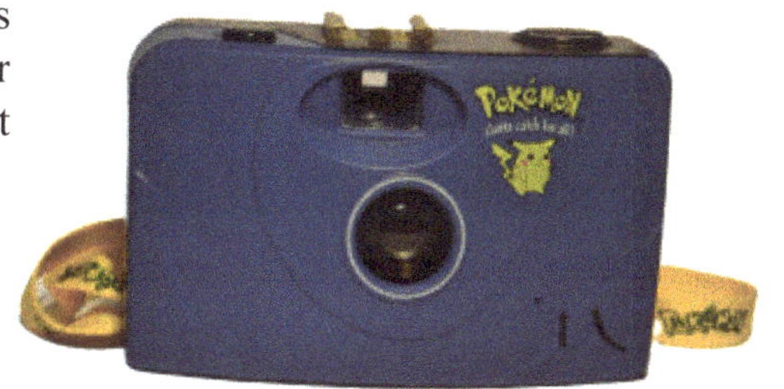

$15-$30

Tiger Electronics, Ltd. was acquired by Hasbro Toy Company, Inc. in 1998.

Pokemon Disposable Camera—Japan (2000)

This camera came packed in a box with Pokemon characters printed all over it. The camera uses 35mm roll films and has an electronic flash. This is a cheap camera with a plastic body with a cardboard covering depicting Pokemon characters. However the language printed on the camera covering is Japanese.

$15-$30

Pichu & Pikachu 35mm Flash Camera (2001)

This plastic camera is gold in color and has Pichu & Pikachu printed on the right front while Pikachu and friends are illustrated on the left. This camera was a commemorative one for the Pokemon movie "Pikachu The Movie 2001: Pikachu & Pichu." As the movie goes, Pikachu visits the big city with his Pokemon buddy Pichu to celebrate his birthday.

The camera uses 35mm roll films and has a 27mm wide angle lens, single-speed shutter and built-in electronic flash. Copyrighted by Nintendo/Creatures Inc. and Game Freak Inc., it is considered rare.

$400-$600

Pokemon Pikachu Flash Camera (1999)

This camera is yellow and larger than most and has the "Pokemon" logo on the front of the camera, with the slogan, "Gotta Catch 'Em All" directly under it. The camera uses 35mm roll films and has a built-in electronic flash powered by a single AA battery.

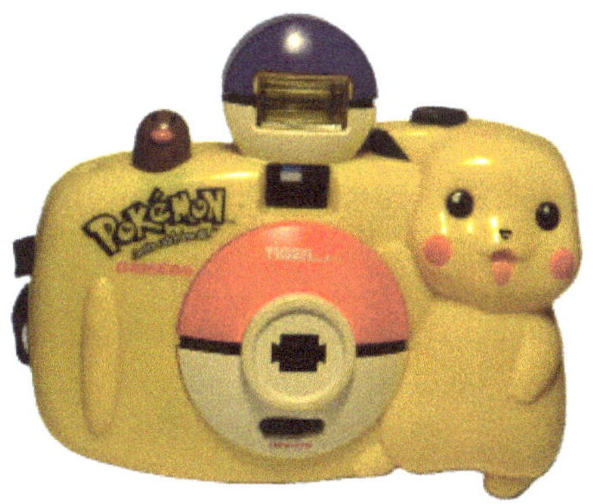

The hallmark of this model is that every time you take a picture a special Pokemon border with all 150 Pokemon "magically appears" on each photo. The Pikachu character figures prominently as part of the camera body. The original list price for this camera was $13.86 in 1999. It was manufactured under license for Nintendo by Tiger[1] Electronics, Ltd., USA (parent Hasbro, Inc.). It was made in China.

$25-$50, camera only; $90-$150, in original packaging

Pokemon Pikachu Polaroid I-Zone Camera (1999)

This is a "special markets" camera produced by Polaroid for Nintendo. This one is yellow and white and has Pikachu on its face.

These cameras used a special Polaroid instant "Pocket Film." Although the picture size is the same as that of 35mm film (24x36mm), they don't use regular 35mm films. The films for the I-Zone models were discontinued in 2006.

Other features were a focus-free lens, a built-in selectable flash, and manual film advance. The power source is two AA batteries unlike so many of the Polaroid cameras that had the power source built-in to the film pack.

$80-$125

Pokemon Shogakukan Camera – Japan (1999)

A yellow camera with a plastic body that opens by splitting the halves in front to expose the lens and view-finder. It uses 35mm roll films and has a hot shoe for a flash. The front of the camera depicts Pokemon characters. Copyrighted by Nintendo/Creatures. Inc., and Game Freak Inc.

$50-$120

Pokemon Shogakukan Panorama Camera—Japan (1998)

This was reportedly a handout promotion at a Nintendo convention in 1998 at the Shogakukan Convention Center in Japan. It features a printed Pikachu character on the face. It has a f/9.6, 28mm fixed-focus lens that can be set for either normal or panorama picture mode, with a simple single speed shutter. There is no built-in flash but there is a hot shoe. It uses 35mm roll films and with a suggested film speed range between ISO 100-400. Copyrighted by Nintendo/ Creatures Inc., and Game Freak, Inc.

$60-$120 +/-

Pokemon Shogakukan "The Movie" Camera—Japan (1996)

This model was made to commemorate one of the Pokemon movies and has Pikachu and other Pokemon characters featured in a nicely designed strong relief on the face of the camera. It was released in Japan. Uses 35mm roll films, is reusable, and has a hot shoe for an electronic flash. Copyrighted Nintendo/Creatures Inc., and Game Freak Inc.

$150-$200

Pokemon Translucent Camera (1998)

A see-through version of a Pokemon camera with built-in electronic flash and 27mm wide angle lens. It uses 35mm roll films and is reusable. It features a Pikachu character on its face. Copyrighted Nintendo/Creatures Inc., and Game Freak Inc.

$200+/-

Pokka Coffee 35mm Camera (1990s-2000s)

A all black plastic camera with the name Pokka Coffee on face near the optical view-finder. Also has a sticker depicting a person's image and states "Pokka Coffee" all around the sticker. Their logo is also present. The camera was not for sale and presumably was/is a promotional hand-out for purchasing their products and advertising purposes. It has a focus free lens and simple one-click shutter. No flash and uses 35mm roll films. It is licensed by Pokka Corp. (Singapore) PTE. LTD., and made in China.

$5-$15

The Pokka Corporation (Singapore) PTE. LTD. was established in 1977.

Their first product was canned coffee produced in their Singapore factory. However, they did put out a line of canned coffees starting in 1972 under the Pokka name while still being known as the Pokka Lemon Co. LTD. Pokka products are now exported to over 50 countries. In addition, Pokka owns and operates over 700 vending machines in Singapore dispensing their brand of coffees and teas.

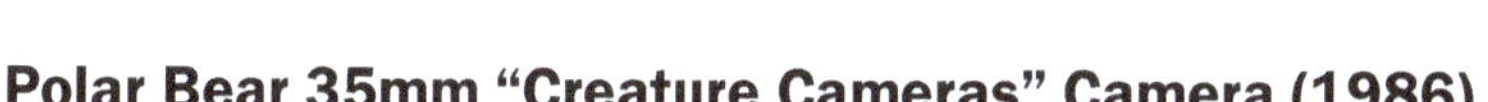

More history here: https://www.pokka.co/about-us/history

Polar Bear 35mm "Creature Cameras" Camera (1986)

This camera is from the "Creature Camera" series by Kids Can Press and licensed by Provincial Products, Inc. It was part of their promotion of "Franklin the Turtle" book series and books about "Elliot Moose".

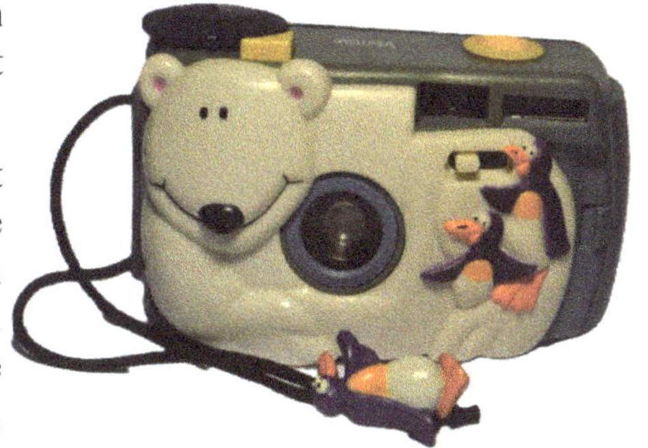

There is a large relief image of a Polar Bear on front of camera and a penguin on the carry strap. Simple one click shutter and focus free lens and uses 35mm roll films. Flash models require two AAA batteries. Other "Creature Camera" series cameras include Franklin the Turtle, Batman & Robin, Alligator, Monkey, Cat & Mouse, Crocodile, Sesame Street, Rugrats, and famous Looney Tunes characters. It is manufactured in China by Vivitar Corporation; ©Provincial Products, Inc.; Uncommon.

$20-$50

Kids Can Press, Toronto, Ontario is a children's book publishing company.

Polly Pocket 35mm Camera (1998)

This plastic 35mm reusable camera has no flash. It comes in various colors including a translucent one. It has "Polly Pocket" printed on the sliding lens cover. Copyrighted Bluebird Toys (UK), Ltd., it was made in China. It is fairly common.

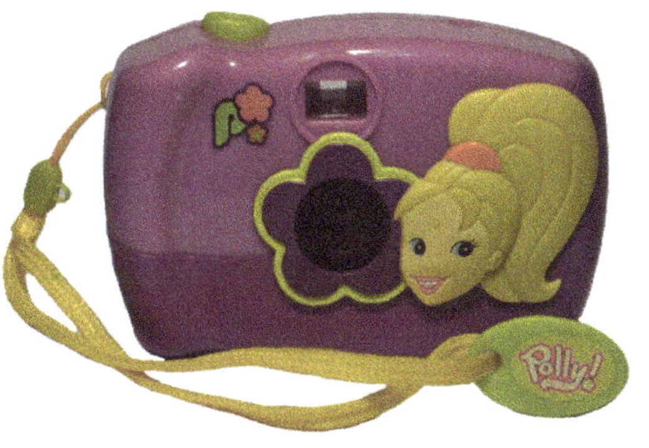

$5-$15

Polly Pocket Outdoor Camera (1998)

This is a cheap camera with a plastic body and a colorful cardboard covering with a picture of Polly in a heart frame and the words Polly Pocket with a heart on top front. It has no flash and comes preloaded with 24-exposure, ISO 100, 35mm color film. Copyrighted by Bluebird Toys (UK), LTD., it was made in China. It is uncommon.

$25-$50, realistic pricing although an asking price of $324 was seen on eBay

Polly Pocket 35mm Outdoor Camera Kit (2004)

This Polly Pocket camera was manufactured in China by Origin Products, Ltd., under license by Mattel, Inc. The outfit came with a "Polly Pocket Styled" body and carry strap, a "Polly" photo album, a frame to put favorite pictures in, and a 12-exposure roll of 35mm "Polly Pocket Film." It has a simple one-click shutter, focus-free lens and comes in various colors. It was distributed by KIDdesigns, Warlingham, England, and is fairly common.

$1-$10, camera only; $15-$30 in original packaging

Polly was first designed by Chris Wiggs in 1983 for his daughter Kate and originally sold by Bluebird Toys of Swindon, England. In the early 1990s, Mattel, Inc., held a distribution arrangement with Bluebird Toys for Polly Pocket items. Mattel purchased Bluebird Toys in 1998.

the *POWER RANGERS* section

Power Ranger 110 Flash Camera (1993)

This pocket camera comes in various colors and has the Red Power Ranger in heavy relief on front. It uses type 110 cartridge films and has an electronic flash requiring one AA battery to operate. Copyrighted by The Walt Disney Corp., it was made in China.

$5-$15, camera only; $20-$40, in original packaging

Power Rangers 110 Camera—Japan (1990)

An unassuming plastic pocket camera that uses 110 cartridge films. It has the Red Power Ranger mounted on front as a lens cover and has a sticker with other Power Rangers on top of the camera. It has a simple one-click shutter and no flash. It was made in Japan.

$50-$90

Power Rangers Adventure/Mission Kit (2014)

The kit included a reusable 35mm camera, flashlight, and binoculars. Camera has a focus-free lens and simple one-click shutter, with no flash. All items in the kit are covered with depictions of Power Ranger characters.

$5-$15, camera only; $20-$40, in original packaging

Power Rangers PuriPachi Japanese Camera (1998)

This camera features The Power Rangers Galactic Warrior Gingaman in a heavy relief design on face. It comes preloaded with 27 exposures, ISO 400; 35mm color print film. The lens is focus free and the shutter is a simple one-click operation. It also has a built-in optical viewfinder but no flash. This camera was released in Japan by the Bandai Company, Ltd., Tokyo, Japan, and made in China. It is highly collectible and sought after by both camera and Power Rangers collectors alike. Bandai Company is a Japanese multinational manufacturer and distributor of toys.

$150-$250

More about Gingaman here: https://en.wikipedia.org/wiki/Seijuu_Sentai_Gingaman

And here as well: https://powerrangers.fandom.com/wiki/Seijuu_Sentai_Gingaman

Power Rangers Mighty Morphin Disposable Flash Camera (2002)

A cheap plastic disposable indoor/outdoor flash camera, it comes preloaded with a 24-exposure, 35mm color print film. It was made in China.

$15-$25, camera only; $30-$55, in original packaging

Power Rangers Ninji Storm Single-Use Flash Camera (2003)

A plastic single-use camera with three Power Rangers featured on the face: the Yellow, the Red, and the Blue. It comes preloaded with a 27-exposure, 35mm, ISO 800 color print film and has an electronic flash. The film was made in Italy and the camera was made in China. It was distributed by Target Corp. USA.

$5-$15, camera only; $15-$30, in original packaging

Power Rangers S.P.D. Outdoor Camera and Binocular Kit! (2005)

This Power Rangers S.P.D. camera is an inexpensive point and shoot 35mm camera kit that includes a focus-free camera, roll of Kodak 12-exposure, ISO 400, 35mm film, binoculars with 3x power, and 26 stickers to use on photos. It has 3-D "Power Ranger" stickers on both the camera and binoc- 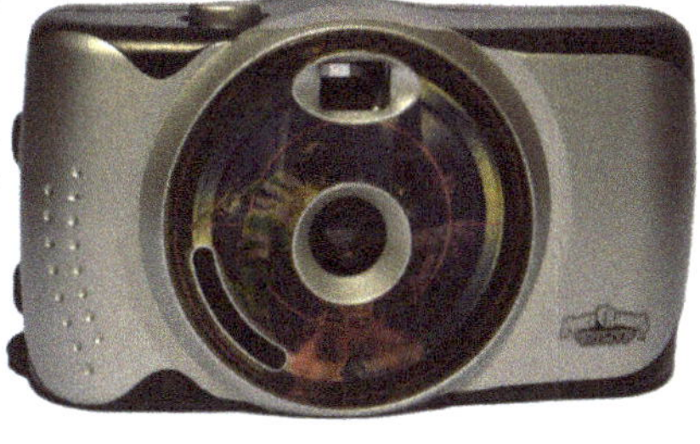 ulars, which appear to move as they are turned in and away from light. It was made in China under license for The Walt Disney Corp., who holds the copyright.

$1-$10, camera only; $10-$20, in original packaging

S.P.D. stands for "Space Patrol Delta." You can find informa-tion about the animated law enforcement agency here: https://bit.ly/PowerRangersSPD 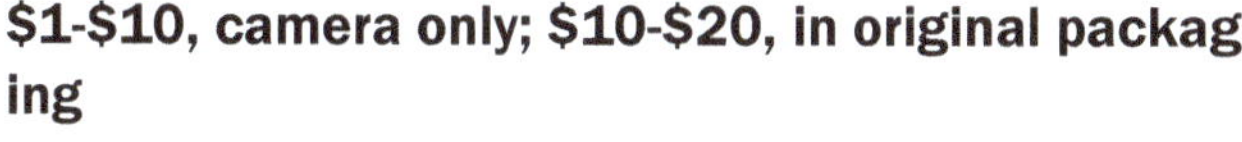

Pro Plan 35mm Camera by Argus (1993)

This plastic camera is fairly stout and came in several colors. It has the Pro Plan brand pet food name and logo printed under lens and uses standard 35mm roll films. Other features include a focus free lens; simple one click shutter; optical viewfinder; and a hot shoe for an electronic flash (no built-in flash). Pro Plan and other brands of pet foods and pet supplies are made by Nestle Purina PetCare based in St. Louis, MO, USA. It was made in China by Argus Photo Corp.

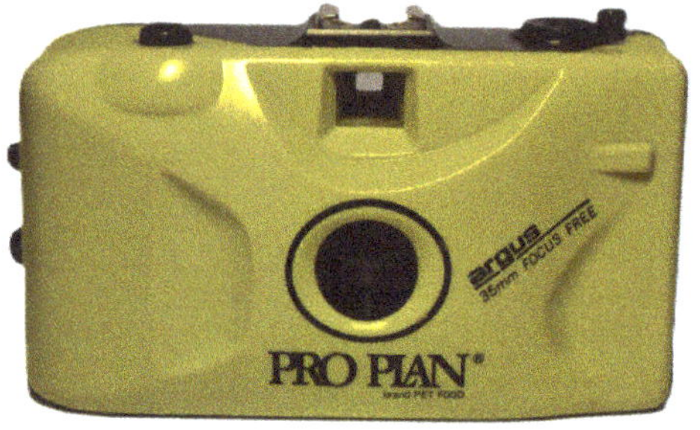

$10-$20

Founded in 1931, Argus was first known as the International Radio Corp. of Ann Arbor, MI, USA, and officially changed their name to Argus in 1944.

However, camera production ended by 1969 but some rebadged cameras were sold into and through the 1970s. In a more recent turn of events the Argus brand has been resurrected and used on a line of cheap digital cameras under the name Argus Camera Company, LLC, Inverness, Illinois, USA.

Punky Brewster 110 Camera (1984)

A plastic all red pocket camera with an odd top cover that pops up. On the cover is a depiction of Punky Brewster with a rainbow, stars, and clouds. There is a decal of her name on the front of the camera beside the lens. It uses type 110 cartridge films, focus-free lens and no flash. Original price for this camera was $5.97. It was made in Taiwan for Helm Toy Corp., and copyrighted by NBC, Inc. It is somewhat uncommon.

$15-$30, camera only; $80-$120, in original packaging

Punky Brewster is a television show about a young girl abandoned by her mother and raised by a single foster male parent. The show aired from 1984-1986 on the NBC network in the United States. https://bit.ly/Punky_Brewster

Quad Cam Four-Lens Camera (2001)

This is a small plastic camera that takes four pictures on a single frame of 35mm film. There are four small wide-angle meniscus lenses and a fly-wheel for a shutter with a 0.22 second delay between each of the four frames. The system is cheap but very effective. The pictures turn out clear and separated on the single frame of film. Reportedly, there is a version of this camera with a real optical viewfinder on top instead of the simple flip-up type. Some older versions had a flip-up wire finder. No flash available so it was recommended that you use ISO 200 or higher speed films. These cameras come in a variety of colors as well as transparent. ©Accoutrements, Seattle, WA. Made in China and marketed under many names. These cameras are still in production.

$12.95 Retail

Older versions w/wire finder: $10-$20

Radio I-Zone Camera by Polaroid (2001-2002)

This I-Zone model is similar to all the I-Zone cameras except it is also a working radio with built-in FM reception (no AM) and has electronic tuning and automatic station search (but has no means of displaying the station being received). It has a headphone jack and no speakers so you need headphones to listen to the radio. Oddly though, the headphones are stereo but the radio is monophonic only; came with a belt-clip but no carry strap. Camera body color came only in translucent teal with yellow trim.

The Camera was sold as a complete kit and included a six-exposure film pack and two AA batteries to power the built-in electronic flash (unlike other Polaroid integral films, this new Pocket Film does not contain its own power source). It has a simple one-click shutter and focus-free lens.

The I-Zone model camera was introduced in 1999 and was originally available in a choice of three bright colors: vibrant green, red, and blue. The film for the I-Zone models was discontinued in 2006. This and other "Special Markets I-Zone" models were actually manufactured for Polaroid by Tomy, a Japanese toy maker. ©Polaroid Corp., Inc.

$15-$50+

Polaroid was purchased by the capital firm One Equity Partners in 2002 who filed bankruptcy in 2008. Holding company PLR IP now controls the Polaroid brand name.

Ragu Single-Use 35mm Camera (1996)

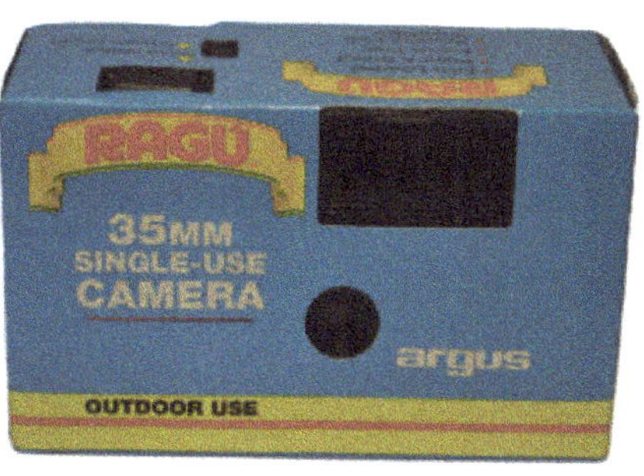

This camera is a typical generic disposable type with a cardboard covering depicting the Ragu Company logo. It comes preloaded with 12 exposure, ISO 100, 35mm color film; no flash. Simple one-click shutter and focus free lens. Manufactured in China by Argus Industries, Inc., IL for Ragu Foods, Inc. This Camera was obtained through a mail-in offer.

$2-$12

Argus first began manufacturing cameras in Ann Arbor, Michigan in 1936 and has, over the years, produced many camera models including movie cameras, movie projectors, slide projectors, even being a leading supplier of military cameras, binoculars, periscopes, and gun sights during WWII. Today, Argus products include a wide variety of digital imaging cameras and video products.

Ragu Foods of Merced, CA is primarily known for their spaghetti sauce and related food products.

Ranger Rick 35mm Camera (2011)

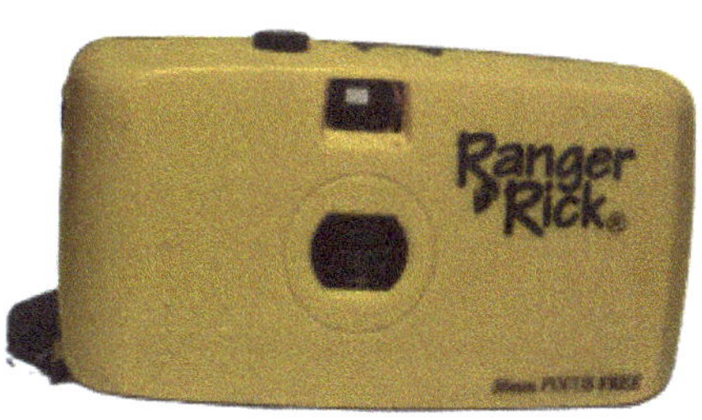

This camera is made of plastic and has a rather unassuming design. It has a yellow front with "Ranger Rick" printed on it. The back is black, and it has a simple lens and viewfinder with a one-click shutter operation, uses 35mm film and no flash. It was made in China.

$1-$10

Ranger Rick is a children's nature and activities magazine first published by the National Wildlife Federation 1967.

RCA Single-Use Camera (2008)

This is a typical plastic body with cardboard covering with the RCA logo printed on the front along with RCA's two iconic dogs. The box notes, "Bonus 30 total exposure," giving the product three free exposures. It comes preloaded with ISO 400, 35mm film, and a battery to power the flash. Distributed and sold by Power Devices, LLC, under license, it is copyrighted by RCA (Radio Corporation of America) Trademark Management, S.A. It was made in China.

$5-$15

Red Baron PhotoAce Camera by Schwan's (1995)

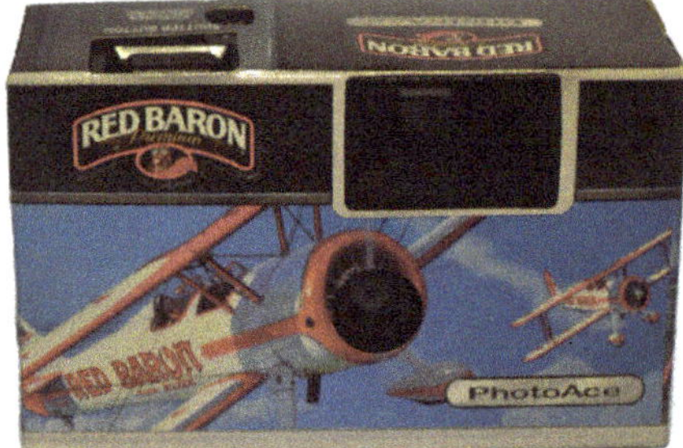

A plastic disposable box camera with a cardboard covering depicting the iconic Red Baron and the fighter plane he used in WWI to promote Schwan's Red Baron brand premium frozen pizzas. It comes preloaded with 12-exposure, ISO 100, 35mm color print film, has a fixed focus f/8 lens, a simple one-click shutter and no flash. Copyrighted by Red Baron Pizza Service, it was made in China.

$2-$12

The famous "Red Baron" of World War 1, Manfred Albrecht Freiherr von Richthofen, was a German Air Force fighter pilot who had over 80 victories during combat. He was shot down and died on April 21, 1918.

Schwan's originated in the United States in 1952 as a family-owned business. However, since 2019 the company has been a subsidiary of CJ CheilJedang of South Korea. Schwan's Company is widely known for its consumer food brands, including Red Baron, Freschetta, Tony's, Mrs. Smith's, Edwards, and Pagoda. For information about the CJ CheilJedang company: https://bit.ly/CJ_CheilJedang

Reese's FBI Jr. Camera (1991)

This plastic 110 cartridge film camera is made to look like a package of two Reese's Peanut Butter Cup candies and was marketed as a "secret agent" toy for kids called the "FBI Jr. Reese's Camera." It also includes a plastic "Junior Special Agent" badge.

There are variations of this camera to look out for, including models with a pop-up viewfinder while others have a thru-the-body built-in finder, and different wrap styles. It retailed for about $10. It was made for Hershey Foods Corporation and licensed by Nasta International, Inc. of New York, NY, USA. It was made in China.

$20-$30, camera only; $40-$50, in original packaging

The H.B. Reese Company (created in 1928 and known for their Peanut butter cups) was sold to the Hershey Company in 1963 for $23.5 million. Reese's is a trademark of Hershey Foods Corporation.

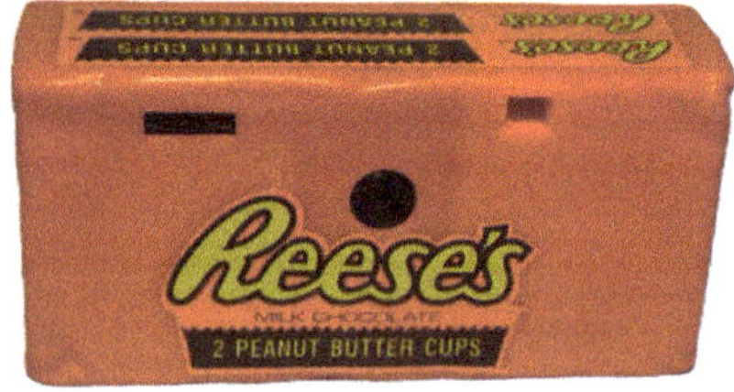

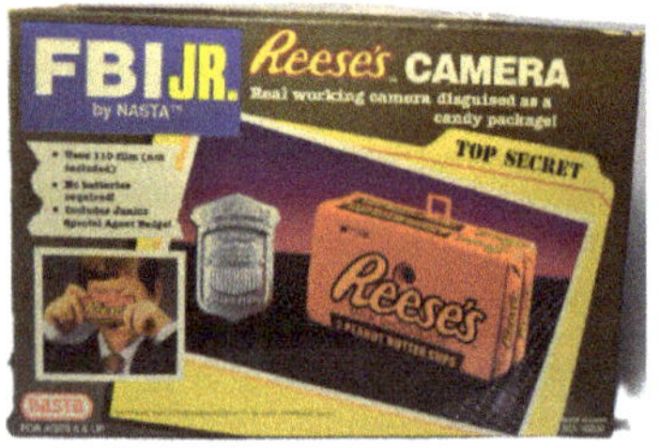

Rugrats 35mm Camera (1998)

This is a reusable 35mm camera that came in two versions, with or without a flash. It has a heavy relief of the Nickelodeon's Rugrats on the face of the camera and a ball on the end of the carry strap. It features a simple one-click shutter and focus-free lens. It requires two AAA batteries to power the flash in those models. Provincial Products (Mattel, Inc.) licensed and produced the cameras for their "Creature Camera" series, which also depict Batman and Robin, a Polar Bear, a Monkey, a Cat and Mouse, a Crocodile, a Caterpillar, as well as Sesame Street and famous Looney Tunes characters, so there are plenty to look out for. It was made in China by Vivitar Corporation for Mattel, Inc.

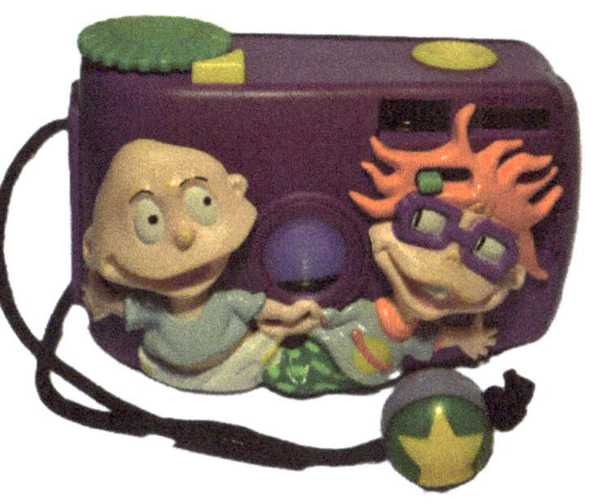

$25-$40

In November 2006, Vivitar Corporation (founded in 1938) was purchased by Syntax-Brillian Corporation. In August 2008, Sakar International of Edison, New Jersey (founded in 1977) acquired Vivitar from Syntax-Brillian Corporation who then filed for bankruptcy the same year.

Rugrats Around The World Camera (2002)

Another disposable camera that was wrapped in a blue cardboard cover with "Rugrats Around The World" on the face. It features a simple shutter and focus-free lens and has a built-in electronic flash. It comes preloaded with 35mm film. It is a hand-out to promote the weekly magazine in the UK. Copyrighted by Viacom International, Inc., it was made in China. It is uncommon.

$125-$175

Rugrats Around The World was a weekly collectors magazine sold in the UK in 2001. The magazines contained history and scientific facts and also included comics and stickers. The magazines came with a folder to store them in, a camera, a Frisbee, and a carry bag. https://bit.ly/RugRats_RTW

At 14 years, Rugrats was Nickelodeon's longest running show. The series was in production from 1991 to 1994, and again from 1996 to 2004. The Rugrats received a star on the Hollywood Walk of Fame on June 28, 2001. In August of that year, the Rugrats celebrated its 10-year anniversary. The show ended in 2004.

Rugrats In Paris Camera (2000)

This cheap disposable camera with a plastic body with a cardboard wrapping and a stamp print that reads "Rugrats In Paris: The Movie" on the face and is a promo handout for the movie. It comes preloaded with 35mm color print film, has a simple one-click shutter, focus-free lens and no flash. It was made in China.

$20-$30

San Francisco Giants Camera (2000s)

A cheap camera with a plastic body and a cardboard wrap-around that has a baseball and "Giants" printed over it. It was a Father's Day game day hosted by Macy's and The San Francisco Chronicle (newspaper) which provided the giveaway to promote the day and themselves. It comes preloaded with a 24-exposure, ISO 200, 35mm color print film. It has no flash. It was made in China.

$12-$25

Sara Lee Single-Use Outdoor Camera (1990s)

This camera is not only a disposable, single-use camera, it's a recycled one as well: the cardboard covering notes that it is a recycled, reloaded, repackaged product. This is one of those

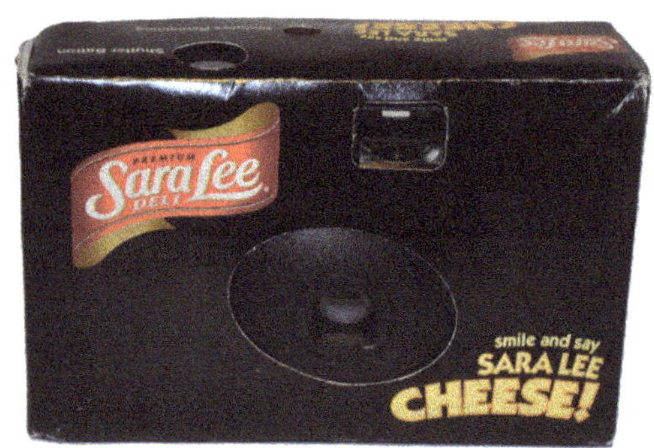

generic plastic camera bodies that companies cover with their logos and use as giveaways to promote their products. This one is covered in black cardboard with the "Sara Lee" logo printed on it and comes preloaded with a 20-exposure roll of ISO 200, 35mm film (manufactured in Germany). It had no flash, a Simple one-click shutter and focus-free lens. Licensed by Sara Lee Corp., and distributed by Concept Marketing, Grand Rapids, MI, USA. It was made in China.

$1-$10

Formally the C.D. Kenny Company: Founded in 1939, becoming Consolidated Grocers Corporation in 1945, and Consolidated Foods Corporation in 1954, then changed its name to Sara Lee Corp., in 1985. You may have enjoyed one of their pies.

Say Cheese Indoor-Outdoor Camera (1994)

This ready-to-use point and shoot camera features Brett Farve (#4) of the National Football League's Green Bay Packers team. The package notes that the first photo on roll is an autographed photo of Farve. It comes preloaded with 26-exposure, 35mm, ISO 400 color print film, and a battery for the flash. It was made in the United States by Sundance Photo, Inc., of Jackson, WI, USA. It is considered rare.

$200-$400

Brett Farve played quarterback for the Green Bay Packers for most of his football career and appeared with them in two Super Bowl games and winning Super Bowl XXXI and losing Super Bowl XXXII. In his 17-year NFL career, Farve went on to play with other teams like the NY Jets and the Minnesota Vikings, before he retired.

Much more about Brett Farve here: https://bit.ly/BrettFarve

Farve's profile on the Pro Football Hall of Fame: https://bit.ly/Farve_ProHOF

Say Cheese! Camera (1990s)

Dubbed the Chuck E Cheese Camera (but they are wrong)

This cute reusable 35mm camera is reputed by many to be Chuck E Cheese on the front. But they are wrong and this is why: Repeated searches for images of the Chuck E Cheese mouse character never show him without clothing of some sort. Furthermore, he also wears a hat with his initial "C" on cap. Sometimes a picture of him without his cap pops up, but virtually every picture of him is with his cap.

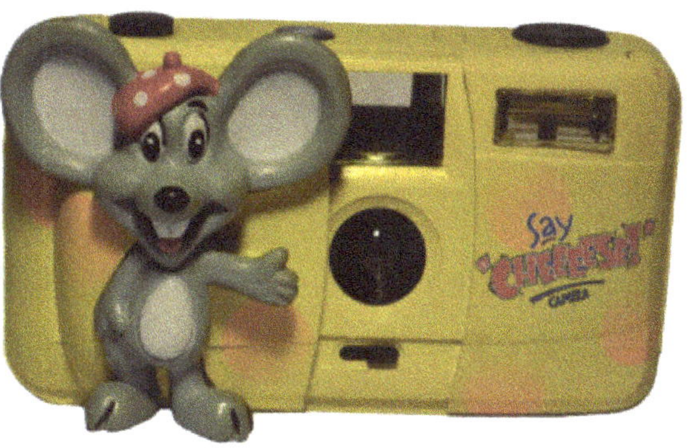

Another odd thing is that there is no logo or mention of Chuck E Cheese on the camera. If this were really a Chuck E Cheese camera one would think they would want us all to know for sure. That's just good advertising. And last but not least, this camera states on front it is the "Say Cheese! Camera."

Uses any standard 35mm roll-films and has an electronic flash requiring one AA battery to operate. It has a simple fixed focus lens and one-click shutter operation. Mouse character is mounted on sliding door that covers lens and large optical viewfinder when not in use. It is made in China. No matter what you call it it's a great collectible.

$30-$50

Secret Sam Spy Camera Kit (1965)

This boxy camera came in a kids spy kit that included the camera, a pistol (that shoots long or short bullets), a periscope, a silencer (for pistol), and a message missile (that also shoots from the pistol); all in a heavy vinyl attaché case. Both the camera and pistol could be used while in the case. The camera could also be used outside the case by itself and uses No. 127 roll films for 16 exposures (still available). This camera spy kit is rare to find in its complete form. The camera by itself will be easier to come by. ©De Luxe Reading Corp., Elizabeth, NJ, USA; and made by Topper Toys in the USA.

$20-$40 camera alone; $300-$500 entire, intact, kit

Sesame Street 110 Flash Camera Kit (1998)

The box of this kit has Big Bird pictured on it as well as on the photo album in the kit. The camera has Elmo pictured on top and front and came with one 12 exposure, ISO 200, Kodak Gold 110 film cartridge, two AA batteries to power electronic flash, and a photo album. Simple lens and one-click shutter operation. ©Children's Television Workshop; ©Jim Henson Company; marketed and distributed by Jazz Photo Corp., Carteret, NJ, USA; and made in China.

$15-$25 camera alone; $40-$65 kit in original packaging.

Sesame Street 35mm Single-Use Camera (1998)

This disposable camera celebrates Sesame Street's "30 years and counting" anniversary and has Big Bird pictured on the box and features Grover on the face of camera. It comes preloaded with 27 exposure, ISO 400, 35mm Kodak Gold color print film; optical viewfinder and electronic flash, including battery for flash. ©Children's Television Workshop; ©Jim Henson Company; marketed and distributed by Jazz Photo Corp., Carteret, NJ, USA; and made in China.

$25-$40

Sesame Street Creature Camera Outfit (1998)

This reusable camera outfit includes a 35mm camera, photo album (which holds 40 prints), a roll of 35mm color film (ISO 400), and two AAA batteries to power the flash. It features the Elmo character in heavy relief on the face of the camera. It was produced by Provincial Products, Inc., and copyrighted by Jim Henson Company. It was made in China.

$50-$100

Sesame Street Elmo 110 Model S-100 Camera (1998)

This basic 110 film cartridge camera with a flash features one of Sesame Street most famous characters, Elmo. It is red with a picture of Elmo's face on front of the camera. The top also has Elmo waving hello. The shutter button is green and has the "Sesame Street" logo just above it. It is a simple one-click shutter and focus-free lens. The outfit came with one roll of Scotch Imation film that is rated at ISO 200 and two Kodak brand AA batteries. It was made in China and licensed by The Jim Henson Company, now The Muppets Studio, LLC. (formed in 2004), a wholly owned subsidiary of media conglomerate The Walt Disney Co., who holds the copyright. These are available in various colors. Demand for these is from both camera collectors and Sesame Street fans.

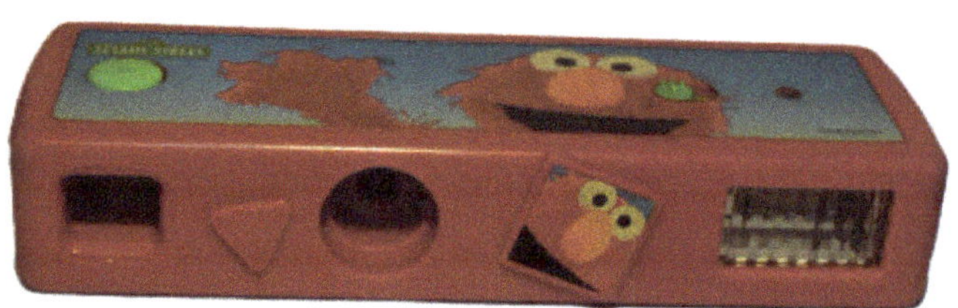

$15-$30, camera only; 50% more in original packaging

Sesame Street is one of the most highly regarded, and most watched, educational shows for children on the planet.

She-Ra Princess of Power Camera (1985)

This is a most interesting designed camera in the form of a castle; Crystal Castle. It is pink, adorned with gold and the "She-Ra Princess of Power" character stands to one side ready for action; all in heavy molded relief. This Masters of the Universe camera used type 110 film cartridges and X-type flash cubes. Original selling price was $9.97 and was produced by HG Toys, LTD., Long Beach, NY, USA. ©Mattel, Inc. and made in China and is uncommon, perhaps rare.

$150-$225 camera alone or with original packaging in poor condition;

$250-$350 with original packaging in good or better condition.

Collector's note: *A green/gray He-Man 110 camera, Castle Grayskull, was also released in 1985.*

the *Simpsons* section

Simpsons 35mm Camera (1997)

This is a green plastic camera with Homer and Bart in heavy relief on the face. It has Hanimex printed on top. It uses 35mm roll-films and features a simple one-click shutter and plastic lens. It was made in China.

$80-$120

Fuji Film Company acquired Hanimex from NRG Overseas Investment Ltd. of Ricoh Company, Ltd. in 2004. The Hanimex name was then discontinued. In its day Hanimex sold cameras, lenses, projectors. Much more found here: https://bit.ly/Hanimex-Wiki

Simpsons Quick-Snap Outdoor Camera (2000)

A camera with a plastic body and a cardboard wrap around cover that features Bart, Lisa, Otto the bus driver, and friend Millhouse on the face. The single use camera uses 35mm roll-film and has no flash. This is a premium to promote Barqs Root Beer. Copyrighted by Twentieth Century Fox Corp., and Fuji Film Photo Co., it was made in Japan.

$15-$30

Originally called the Barq's Bottling Company, founded in 1890. Near the beginning of the 20th century, the company began making and bottling its now famous root beer. Barq's was bought and is now owned by the Coca-Cola Co.

More here: https://bit.ly/BarqsWiki

The Barq's history site: https://bit.ly/BarqsHistory

Simpsons Single-Use camera (2003)

The camera face has the Simpson family depicted against a plaid background. It comes pre-loaded with 27-exposure, ISO 800 speed, 35mm color print film and has a built-in electronic flash. The camera body was made in China and the film in Italy. It was distributed by Target Corp., and copyrighted by Twentieth Century Fox Corp.

$15-$30

Simpsons Spy Camera (2004)

A mini camera that uses 110 cartridge films. Copyrighted by Twentieth Century Fox Corp., it was made in China.

$10-$25

Simpsons Underwater 35mm Disposable Camera (1999)

The body of this camera is red and shows Bart lounging on the beach with a cool drink. It comes preloaded with 27-exposure, ISO 400, 35mm color print film. Copyrighted by Twentieth Century Fox Corp., it was made in China.

$15-$30

Simpsons Underwater Single-Use Outdoor Camera (1999)

This is a cheap plastic camera for taking photos underwater. It features Homer Simpson on the face looking toward the sun with a surfboard in his hand. It comes preloaded with 35mm color print film and features a simple one-click shutter plastic lens and no flash. It is copyrighted by Twentieth Century Fox Corp.

$15-$30

Smile 35mm Flash Camera (1980s-90s)

This fairly well built mostly green colored camera states "Smile!" on face and top of body. Just

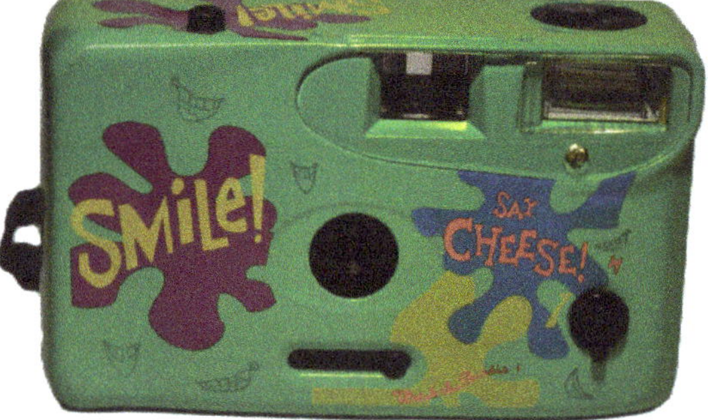

under the flash is stated "Say Cheese!" and near the lens cover control it states "Watch the Birdie!" It uses 35mm roll films and is reusable. The lens is 25mm, f/8; the shutter speed is 1/00th sec.; optical viewfinder; and electronic flash (requires one type AA battery); made in China.

$5-$15

https://www.notes.nicefilmclub.com/ posts/6-weirdest-35mm-cameras

the Snoopy section

Peanuts Beagle Scouts F-11 Camera (2024)

The now famous cartoon comic strip "Peanuts" was created by Charles Schulz in 1950 and this camera is made to celebrate the 50th anniversary of the "Peanuts Beagle Scouts" which he debuted in 1974. Schulz died in 2000. On the face of the camera find Snoopy leading his troops on a journey.

This camera comes with a 31mm, f/9, fixed focus lens; a 1/120 sec. shutter speed; electronic flash (requires 1-AAA battery); and uses standard 35mm roll films with ISO 200 and 400 recommended. ©United Feature Syndicate, Inc. and made by Retrospekt, Milwaukee, WI, USA. This is a limited edition camera.

$40-$80 depending on source seller.

Snoopy 35mm Camera (1990s)

A plastic camera that is a light-blue color with Snoopy printed on front along with him and his buddy Woodstock surf boarding. It uses standard 35mm film and has a hot shoe for a flash unit. Copyrighted by United Feature Syndicate, Inc., it was made in Japan. It is uncommon.

$150-$200

Snoopy Can Camera (1990s)

This unusual camera is in the shape of a soda can. It is red and has "World Famous Beagle" printed on it. It also has Snoopy and his friend Woodstock on the can. It uses 110 cartridge films. It is copyrighted by United Feature Syndicate, Inc.

$50-$100

Snoopy and Charlie Brown 35mm Flash Camera (1998)

Darker blue camera body with images of Charlie Brown reading a newspaper and Snoopy interacting with Woodstock on the face. It uses 35mm roll film and has an electronic flash. Copyrighted by United Feature Syndicate, Inc., it was made in China.

$20-$50

Snoopy Joe Cool Camera (2000s)

This is an all black camera body with an image of Snoopy in his Joe Cool sunglasses on the front. Above the words, "Joe Cool," reads "Nobody knows how tough it is to be this cool." Uses 35mm roll films and has electronic flash. 35mm lens. Copyrighted United Feature Syndicate, Inc.

$80-$150

Snoopy Leica C11 Camera (2023)

Another all black camera with an image of Snoopy on the face taking a photograph of his buddies. This is a much newer camera, with electronic flash, auto-exposure, and an electric film drive. It has a Vario 23-70mm powered lens and uses 35mm roll films. It is made by Leica in Japan.

$700-$800

Snoopy-Matic Instant Camera (1958, 1966)

This camera is shaped like Snoopy's dog house and Snoopy is mounted on the roof. It uses 126 cartridge films and Magic cubes for flash shots. It is licensed and manufactured by Eastman Kodak Company and distributed by Helm Toy Corp. Copyrighted by United Feature Syndicate, Inc., it was made in Hong Kong.

$30-$50, camera only; $100-$150 in original packaging

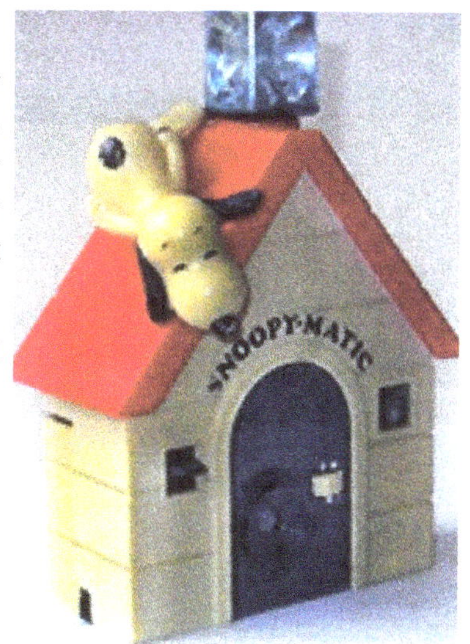

Snoopy Mini Konica Disposable Camera (2000s)

This small plastic camera features Snoopy in his Red Baron outfit on the face. It comes pre-loaded with ISO 400, 24-exposure, 35mm film, with no flash. Copyrighted by United Feature Syndicate, Inc., it was made in Japan.

$20-$40

Snoopy/Peanuts Disposable Camera (2009)

A cheap camera with a plastic body and a cardboard wrap-around covering that features both Snoopy and Charlie Brown on the front. The word "Peanuts" is printed on the face with Snoopy sitting above it. It has electronic flash, fixed-focus lens, one-speed shutter and comes preloaded with 27-exposure, 35mm roll film. It was copyrighted by United Feature Syndicate, Inc., and it was made in China.

$10-$20

Snoopy/Peanuts 35mm Camera Outfit (1990s)

This all white camera body has an image of Snoopy lying on top of his dog house with Charlie Brown resting against the house. It uses 35mm roll film, has a 35mm focus-free lens and there is a hot shoe for a flash. The outfit came with binoculars. It is also available in various colors. Copyrighted by United Feature Syndicate, Inc., it was made in Japan.

$30-$50, camera only; $50-$90 in original packaging

the **SPIDER-MAN** section

Spider-Man 2 Four Piece Camera Kit (2004)

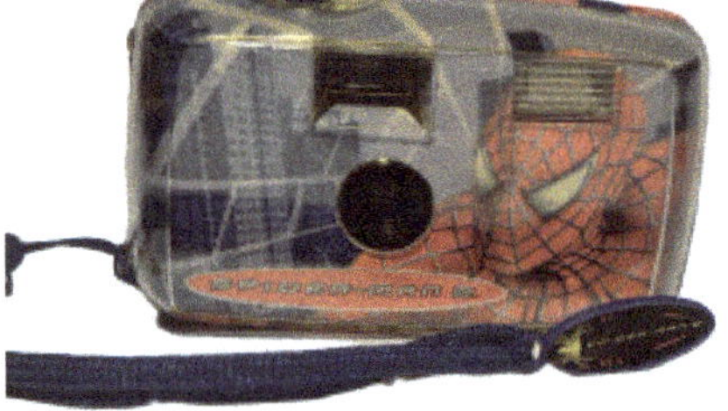

Kit included a 35mm camera, film, battery, and album. This kit is considered official movie merchandise and was used to promote the movie Spider-Man 2. Copyrighted by Marvel Characters, Inc., and distributed by KIDdesigns, Inc., of Rahway, NJ, USA.

$10-$20, camera only; $50-$100, in original packaging

Spider-Man 60th Anniversary Flash Camera (2022)

A rather unassuming camera with all the graphics located on the back of the camera body. This is a single-use camera and comes preloaded with 36-exposure, ISO 400, 35mm color print film. It was made in China under license and copyrighted by Marvel Characters, Inc.

$40.00 +/- retail

Spider-Man Camera (1978)

The original Spider-Man camera is made of plastic and uses 126 cartridge films, flash cubes for flash pictures and has a focus-free lens. Copyrighted by Marvel Comics Group and produced by Vanity Fair, it was made in Hong Kong.

$25-$45, camera only; $65-$110 in original packaging

Spider-Man Disposable 35mm Camera (2000s)

A cheap camera with a plastic body and a cardboard wrap-around with a Spider-Man image on it. It comes preloaded with 35mm, ISO 400 color print film, and a battery for the flash. Copyrighted Marvel Characters, Inc., it was made in China.

$5-$15

Spider-Man Edge Of Time Disposable (2011)

This plastic 35mm single-use camera with flash was used to promote the Edge of Time action-adventure video game, based on the Marvel superhero Spider-Man. It comes preloaded with a roll of 35mm print film and battery for the flash. Copyrighted by Marvel Characters, Inc., it was made in China.

$10-$20

Spider-Man Embassy Suites Camera (2004)

This reusable 35mm camera was given as a premium for checking into Embassy Suites Hotel and to promote the movie Spider-Man 2. It has a focus-free lens and no flash. Copyrighted by Marvel, Inc., and Hilton Hospitality, Inc., it was made in China.

$5-$15

Spider-Man Ultimate Message Camera (2002)

An all plastic camera body with a cardboard covering depicting Spider-Man. "Ultimate Spider-Man" is printed below flash. Every photograph taken with this camera has a "Full color Spider-Man border on every picture," plus there are three mystery photos already pre-exposed on the roll of film. It comes preloaded with 24-exposure, ASA 400, 35mm color print film (which was made in Germany) and has an electronic flash. The camera is for lower light situations as the package says, "This camera is not intended for use in bright sunlight." Copyrighted by Marvel Characters, Inc., and designed in the United States, it was made by Universal Camera Company. It was licensed by Brickell Licensing, LLC, and distributed by Entertainment Merchandisers of Van Nuys, CA, USA. It was made in China.

$15-$25

Spider-Man Red Camera (2004)

An almost all red camera body, this has a large blue oval around the lens with an image of Spider-Man and the words "Spider-Man" printed on the side. The camera is reusable and uses 35mm roll-films. It has no flash, a focus-free lens and a carry strap. Licensed by Marvel Characters, Inc., it was copyrighted by Marvel Characters, Inc., and distributed by KIDdesign, Inc., Rahway, NJ, USA. It was made in China.

$5-$15

Ultimate Spider-Man 35mm Camera (2004)

This 35mm camera was used to promote Ultimate Spider-Man, a comic book series that started in 2000 and lasted until 2011. Marvel used the series to revamp and modernize their re-imagining of their Marvel characters. The camera body is mostly red with Spider-Man depicted to one side. It has a pop-up finder and no flash.

$5-$15

More info: https://bit.ly/Ultimate_Spider-Man

Split-Cam 35mm Camera (2014)

A special effects 35mm camera incorporating "Image Fusion Technology." This basic cheap point-and-shoot has simple shutter and fixed-focus lens and is made exclusively for Accoutrements, LLC, of Seattle, WA, USA. Camera allows taking normal pictures and then fusing the two together into different combinations. The images can be made into any combo: a man's head on a cow or a friend with the head of a cabbage replacing his! It can be used either horizontally or vertically. It has no flash and no batteries are required. Comes in blister packaging with complete operating instructions. It was made in China.

$5-$25 retail, depending on the source seller

More here: https://bit.ly/accourtrements

Accoutrements, LLC, of Seatle are the same folks that bring us the PopCam, QuadCam, and SquirtCam.

SpongeBob Squarepants Snappy Cam (2004) and SpongeBob Squarepants Splashy Cam (2004)

Here is a plastic single-use camera that came in two colors and is preloaded with 27 exposures "super duper 35mm film" (ISO 400); simple lens and shutter; optical viewfinder. The Snappy Cam is found in either yellow or blue; with or without a flash. The other, the Splashy Cam is also found in those colors plus it can be used underwater or on land. SpongeBob Squarepants is a Nickelodeon production and the camera was distributed by Emerson Radio, Parsippany, NJ, USA; and made in China; ©2004 Viacom International, Inc. There are many versions of SpongeBob Squarepants cameras to be found, and by different manufacturers and distributers, albeit most are single-use cams.

$20-$50

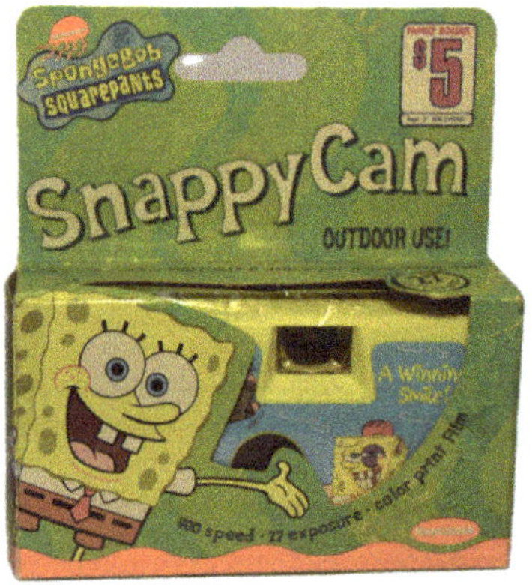
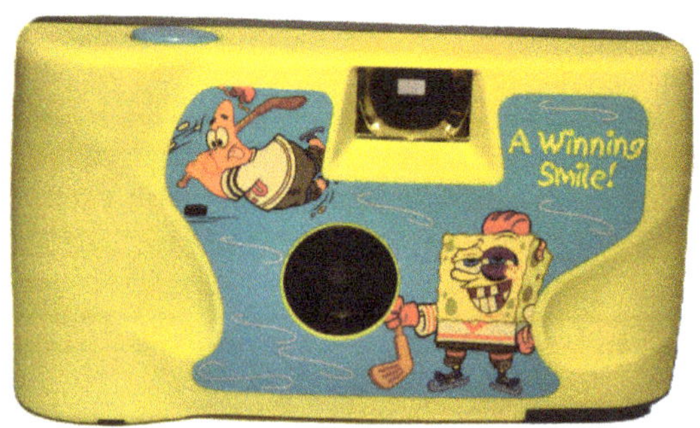

Sports 35 Quad Camera (2001)

This is a small plastic camera that takes four pictures on a single frame of 35mm film. This one has "The Sporting News" printed just below the four lenses; presumably a promotional give-away. A sticker beside the optical viewfinder states "Sports 35". No flash available so it is recommended that you use ISO 200 or 400 speed films. These cameras come in a variety of colors as well as transparent. ©Accoutrements, Seattle, WA. Made in China and marketed under many names. These cameras are still in production

These cameras are still in production. $12.95 retail.

The Sporting News

Serving sports fans since 1886: https://www.sportingnews.com/us

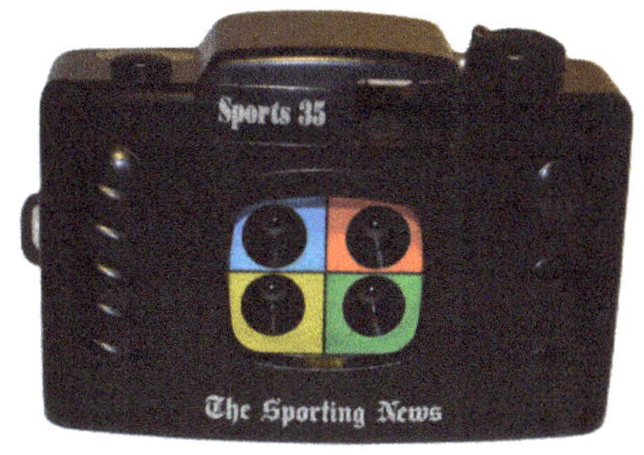

Sports Illustrated 35mm Camera (1985)

This is a plastic 35mm reusable camera that was a give-away premium by Sports Illustrated Magazine for subscribing to receive at least one year of their magazines. It's similar to the Time Magazine camera used for the same purpose. The camera came with a case, lens cap, carry strap, and instruction booklet; no flash but has a hot shoe to add one. In addition, it's equipped with a 50mm, f/6 Kinetic optical color lens, 1/125th sec. shutter, and optical viewfinder; uses standard 35mm roll films with ISO 100 or 200 being the recommended film speeds to use. ©Sports Illustrated, Inc. and made in Taiwan; common.

$5-$15

Spring Break 2003 Message Camera (2003)

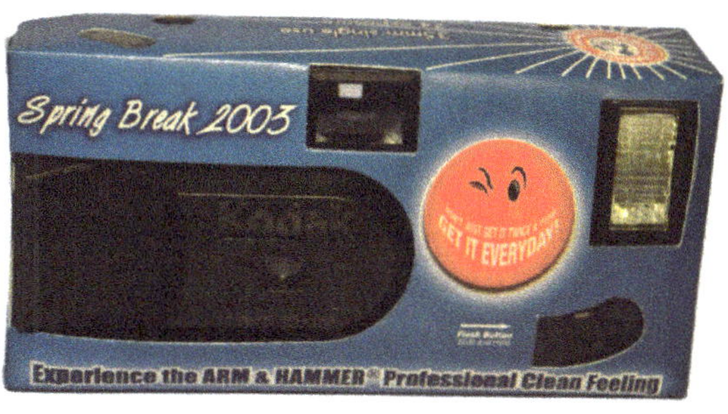

A plastic camera body with a wrap-around cardboard covering promoting Arm & Hammer Advance White Extra Fresh toothpaste. Interestingly, the camera was made by Kodak and the message "Spring Break 2003" appears on every photograph. The camera wrapping itself doesn't indicate the film speed film, but comes preloaded with a 24-exposure, 35mm Kodak film. It has a preset f/11 lens and simple one-click shutter operation with a flash. Licensed by Church & Dwight Co., Inc., it was made in the United States, by Kodak, Inc.

$2-$12

Spy Kids 110 Keychain Camera (2001-2003)

This basic keychain camera was a giveaway with the purchase of a "Kids Happy Meal" by McDonald's Corp., as a promotion during the earlier "Spy Kids the Movie" years. There were three Spy Kids movies made between 2001 and 2003. It retains the general shape of many

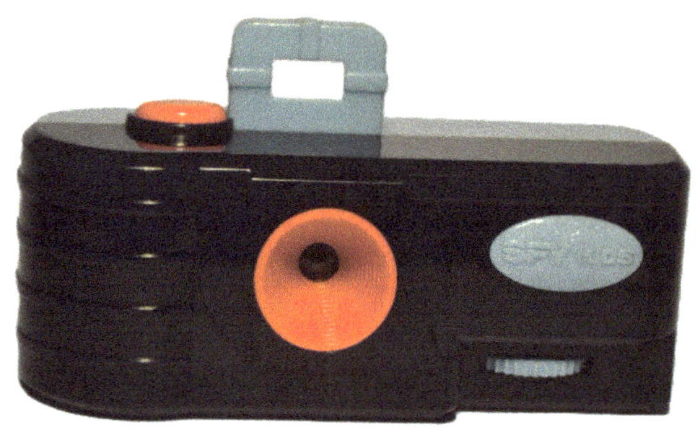

keychain cameras, but is somewhat larger and a rigid viewfinder replaces the typical pop-up viewfinder usually found. It uses 110 cartridge films and requires a coin to open the film door. It is licensed and copyrighted by Miramax Film Corp. for McDonald's Corp., and made in China.

$2-$12

More information: https://bit.ly/SpyKids110

Spy Tech 110 [Hidden] Camera (1989)

The Spy Tech is a real working 110 camera with spy accessories concealed in a secret candy box. The camera came with the Good 'n Plenty candy cover and included a clip on mirror to take pictures around corners. It was made by Tyco Corp., of Princeton, NJ, USA.

$10-$20, camera only; $30-$60, in original packaging

This camera was a part of Tyco's "Spy-Tech," a line of functioning spy equipment made just for kids. The kits include the Commander's Signal Beacon, Security Alarm Case, Periscope, Secret Message Finder Set, Long Range Microphone, Hidden Camera, Digital Fingerprint Kit, and Cracker Jack Periscope. These Spy Tech kits were made between 1989-1992.

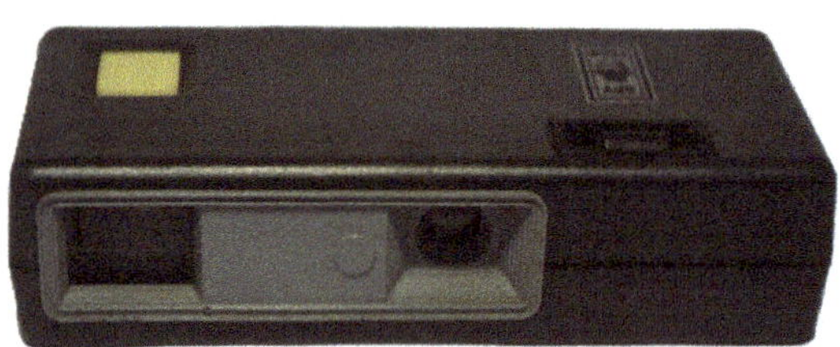

Spy Tech 110 Camera - Front

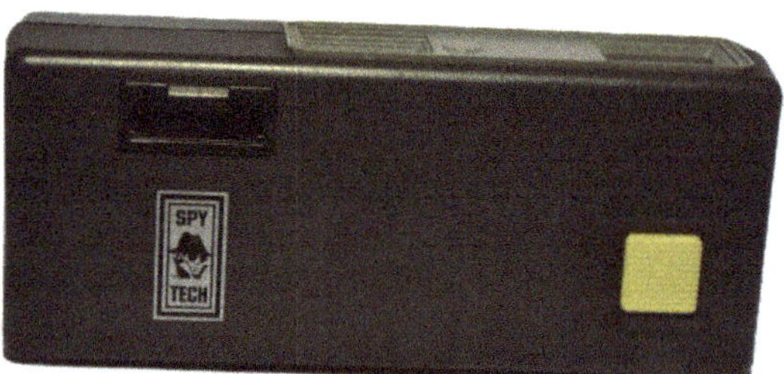

Spy Tech 110 Camera - Top

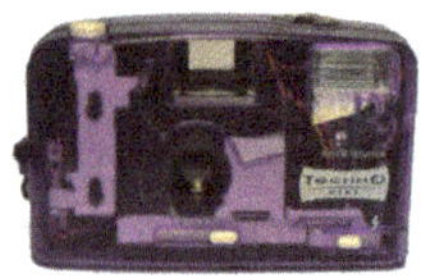

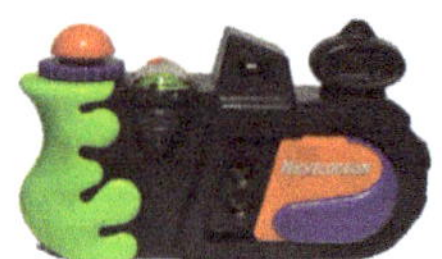

Strawberry Shortcake Fun Flash Camera Combo (2003)

This is a combo set containing a reusable 35mm flash camera, a photo album, and one roll of 12 exposures, ISO 400, Strawberry Shortcake branded 35mm color print film. Other features are a fixed focus lens with sliding protective cover; 1/125 sec. shutter speed; optical viewfinder; and electronic flash requiring one type AAA battery. It is manufactured in China under license by Street Players Holding Corp., Los Angeles, CA, USA; ©2003 Those Characters From Cleveland, Inc.

Complete combo set: $40-$60; Camera alone: $15-$30

Sunoco Flash Camera (2001)

An indoor-outdoor camera with a plastic body and a red cardboard wrap-around covering with starbursts printed on it and the Sunoco logo. It comes preloaded with 27-exposure, ISO 400, 35mm color print film and has a built-in electronic flash. The film is made in Italy and camera in China and it was copyrighted by Sunoco, Inc.

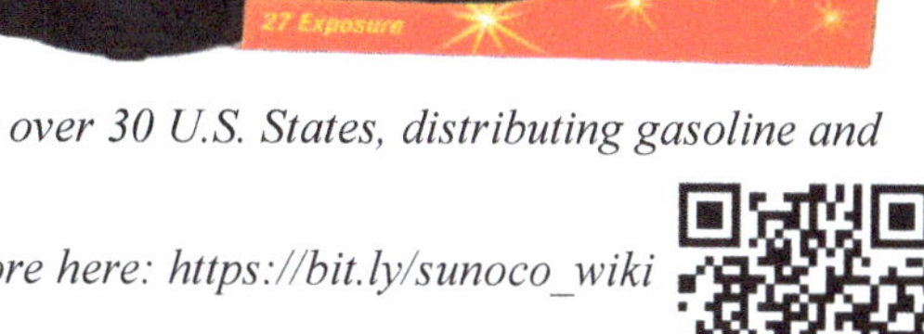

$1-$10

Sunoco (Sun Oil Company) began in Pittsburgh, PA, USA, around 1886. Operated by three partners who already had a gas company called Peoples Natural Gas Company. The Company has been in business for over 130 years. Sunoco has a presence in over 30 U.S. States, distributing gasoline and other fuels.

History: https://bit.ly/aboutsunoco 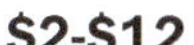 *More here: https://bit.ly/sunoco_wiki*

Superman Returns 35mm Disposable Camera (2006)

This is a rather cheap disposable camera with a printed cardboard cover depicting a great comic book super hero: Superman. This was a promotional giveaway camera for the 2006 movie "Superman Returns" which earned over $391 million. It was also a promotion for Pepsi Cola Corp., Frito-Lay Corp., and The Quaker Oats Co. as they were the main promoters along with others you'll find listed on the front of camera face. However, Warner Brothers decided to shelve the Superman follow-up movie they originally planned for 2009 because they felt the revenues were already too low.

It comes preloaded with a roll of 12 exposure, ISO 100, 35mm color print film (process C-41); optical viewfinder and one-click shutter; no flash. Licensed by ©Warner Brothers Entertainment and made in China. Superman is a registered trademark of D.C. Comics.

$2-$12

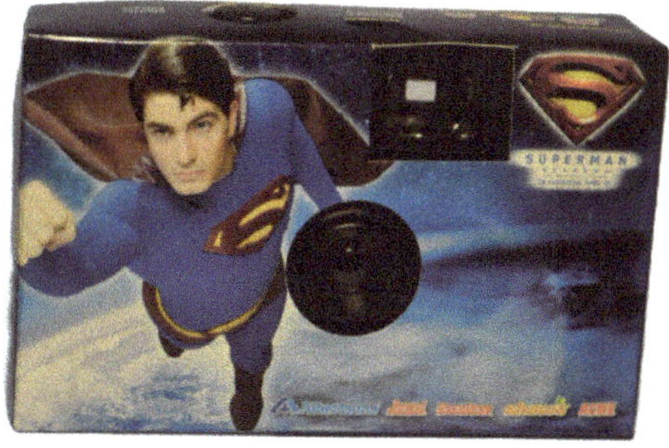

Sylvester & Tweety Mysteries Camera (1997)

A plastic single-use camera with a cardboard wrap-around depicting the Warner Brothers Looney-Tunes cartoon characters Sylvester (the cat) and Tweety (the bird), who is holding a magnifying lens that surrounds the camera lens. "The Sylvester & Tweety Mysteries" is printed on the face. It comes preloaded with 24-exposure, 35mm color print film, with a simple one-speed shutter and no flash. Copyrighted by Warner Brothers, it was made in China.

$10-$20

The Warner Brothers opened their very first theater in 1903 in New Castle, PA, USA, called the Cascade. By 1904 they founded the Duquesne Amusement & Supply Co., based in Pittsburgh, PA, USA, to distribute films to movie houses. Around 1914, they began producing their own films. They incorporated in 1923 around the same time they moved their movie operations to Hollywood, CA, USA. More here: https://en.wikipedia.org/wiki/Warner_Bros.

Warner Brothers Animation produced the Sylvester & Tweety Mysteries TV series. It aired on the Kid's WB channel from September 1995 to February 2000. A total of 52 episodes were made.

Taz 110 Outdoor Camera Kit (1999)

This is a cute Looney Tunes reusable camera featuring Taz the Tasmanian Devil cartoon character on face. The kit came with one cartridge of 12 exposures, ISO 200, Looney Tunes 110 color print film; a "big view" optical viewfinder; a simple one-click shutter and no flash. Other items in the kit include a "Taz" photo album (holds 24-4x6 photos), and 24 stickers to place on your photos; carry strap. ©Warner Brothers, Inc.; and made in China by Kalimar Inc., Chesterfield, MO, USA.

$25-$40 camera alone; $50-80 complete kit in original packaging.

Note: There are three other versions to look for: Bugs Bunny, Tweety Bird, and That's All Folks! featuring Taz, Bugs Bunny, Tweety Bird, Daffy Duck, and Sylvester J. Pussycat together on face.

Taz 35mm Outdoor 35mm Camera Kit (1999)

This is a cute Looney Tunes reusable camera featuring Taz the Tasmanian Devil cartoon character on face. The kit came with one roll of 12 exposures, ISO 100, Looney Tunes 35mm color print film; a "big view" optical viewfinder; a simple one-click shutter and no flash. Other items in the kit include set of (4 x) binoculars, a photo album (holds 24-4x6 photos), 24 bonus stickers to place on your photos, and carry strap. ©Warner Brothers, Inc. and made in China by Kalimar Inc., Chesterfield, MO, USA.

$25-$40 camera alone; $50-80 complete kit in original packaging.

Note: There are three other versions to look for: Bugs Bunny, Tweety Bird, and That's All Folks! featuring Taz, Bugs Bunny, Tweety Bird, Daffy Duck, and Sylvester J. Pussycat together on face.

Taz Instant Camera (1999)

A Polaroid 600 instant camera with the head of the Tasmanian Devil on it. When the camera is in an open position, the Taz shows his teeth. These Polaroid cameras use type 600 instant film and have a 110mm, f/10 fixed lens. Exposures are automatic with speeds of 1/3 to 125th second and have a manual slider control to lighten or darken the photo. Flash is built-in and has a manual override. Battery power is built-in to the film pack as is so many of Polaroid's cameras.

$150-$200

Taz Talking Flash Camera (1999)

This Looney Tunes camera features Taz the Tasmanian Devil cartoon character on the face of camera in relief. The lens is inside Taz's mouth. The camera body is all black with a red button (to fire shutter) and a green button that makes Taz talk and his eyes light up. This camera is one of three to be collected. The other two are a version with the Looney Tunes characters on face around the lens; and a Sylvester & Tweety version. It uses type 110 drop-in cartridge films: has a big optical viewfinder for easy viewing; simple one click shutter and focus free lens. It's made in China by Kalimar, Inc., Chesterfield, MO., USA; ©Warner Bros, Inc.

$10-$20 camera only; $30-$60 in original packaging

Techno Kids Translucent Camera (1990s)

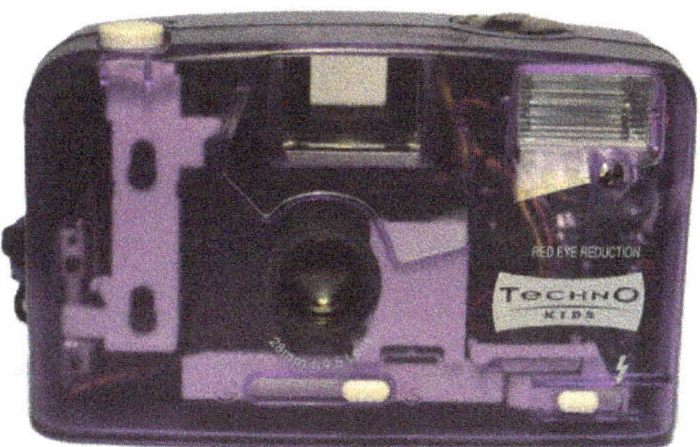

This is a well built reusable plastic purple translucent bodied camera. On the face and under the flash is the Techno Kids name and logo. It uses 35mm roll films; has a large optical viewfinder; a 28mm, f/9.5 lens; one click shutter; and electronic flash (requires one AA battery). It's made in China.

$10-$20

The Techno Kids web site: https://technokids.com/ about-us/

Teenage Mutant Ninja Turtles 35mm Camera (1990)

This camera is a 35mm that comes in various colors with the Turtles faceplate located below the flash and "Teenage Mutant Ninja Turtles" printed on the top of the camera. It features a simple one-click shutter and focus-free lens and uses 35mm roll-films and requires two AA batteries to operate the flash. It was made in China by Remco Toys, New York, NY, USA, and licensed by Mirage Studios USA.

$15-$30

MGM Grand, Inc., and Mirage Resorts, Inc., merged operations on May 31, 2000, forming Mirage Studios USA. They are the exclusive license holders of "Teenage Mutant Ninja Turtles."

Teenage Mutant Ninja Turtles 110 Signature Camera (1990)

This 110 camera was made in China by Remco Toys, Inc., NYC, USA, and licensed by Mirage Studios USA. It has the "Teenage Mutant Ninja Turtles" character "Raphael" on front and came in five colors; orange, green, purple, teal, and yellow.

It used 110 film cassettes but empty cassettes can be reloaded using 16mm film since the camera does not advance the film by way of film perforations. Simple one-click shutter; focus free lens and requires two AA batteries to operate flash (batteries not included with outfit). In addition, each exposure imprints an image of turtle "Michelangelo" into the corner of each print. A carry strap was also included.

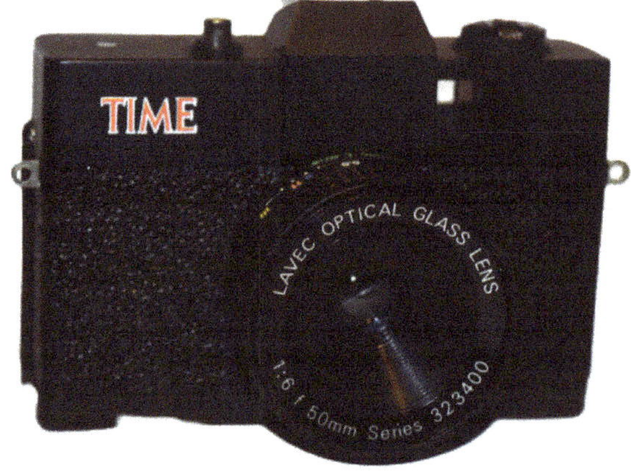

$5-$15 camera only; $15-$30 in original packaging.

Tim Burton's Nightmare Before Christmas Camera (2006-2010)

This is a single-use 35mm, ISO 400, 24 exposure, flash camera that was a promotional tool for the re-release (annually between 2006 and 2010) of the Nightmare Before Christmas presented in Disney Digital 3-D. The camera features 12 different scenes that put you or anyone else in the picture with any one of twelve cast members. The release date for the original movie was October 29, 1993. It's made in USA by License to Play, Inc. Syosset, NY. ©Walt Disney Corp.

$25-$40 (no original box), $45-$55 (with original box)

More information about the Nightmare Before Christmas movie:

https://en.wikipedia.org/wiki/The_Nightmare_Before_Christmas#:~:text=The%20 Nightmare%20Before%20Christmas%20(also,Budget

Time 35mm Camera (1980s)

A cheap 35mm camera given away as a premium by Time Magazine for one year ($20) subscription to the magazine. There are several body style variations and it comes with a case, an instruction booklet and a lens cap. The "TIME" logo is printed on the face of the camera above the lens. It was made in Taiwan.

$1-$10

Tommy Hilfiger Disposable Camera (1997)

A cheap plastic body with a cardboard covering that sports the Tommy Hilfiger logo and colors. It comes preloaded with a 15-exposure, 35mm, ISO 800 color film, and has no flash. It was assembled in the United States from imported and domestic components by Fuji Photo Film, Inc., Greenwood, SC, USA.

$2-$12

Topico Fresh French Fry Camera (1998)

This is a plastic camera in the shape of a red bag of golden French fries and has the Topico logo on face along with "Fresh" printed just above lens. It has a Meniscus 28mm, f/11, fixed focus lens, single-speed shutter, and optical viewfinder; and uses 35mm roll films with ISO 200 or 400 recommended. No flash. It was made in China by Ginfax, Hong Kong, and marketed by Simon Marketing, Int., based in Gloucester, MA, USA.

$25-$50

Trio 3-D Camera (2000s)

This camera has a triple-lens design so that the subject is photographed from three slightly different angles. This one is an automatic 35mm 3D camera and has a motor drive. It also has an electronic flash and requires two AA batteries to operate. Copyrighted by 3D Image Technology, Inc., it was made in China.

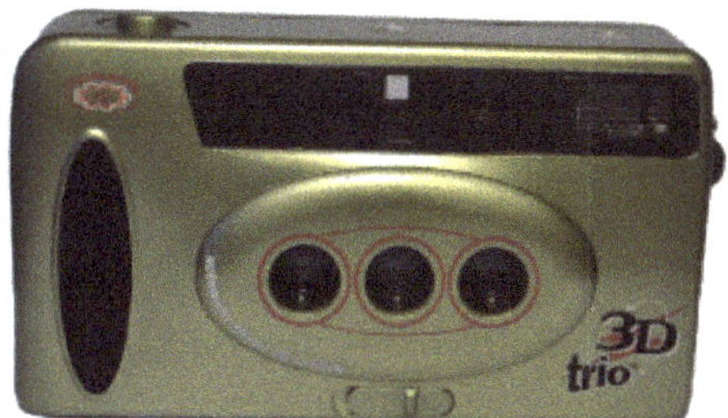

$25-$50

Ukraine Cigarette Spy Camera (2002)

This spy camera was made in the Ukraine as a promo for a brand of cigarettes called "Prima Lux." Made to look like a cigarette pack, it has a 27mm, f9.5 focus-free lens, no flash and uses 35mm roll films. This camera is reported to have been produced in very small quantities as souvenirs for the large Ukrainian tobacco company. And is considered rare.

$150-$200

Underwater Disposable Camera by Wilko (2010)

This camera is for underwater photography and can be used up to 13 feet under the water. Comes preloaded with 24 exposures, ISO 200, color film; no flash; and was/is distributed in the UK by Wilkinson, S80 3YY.

$1-$12

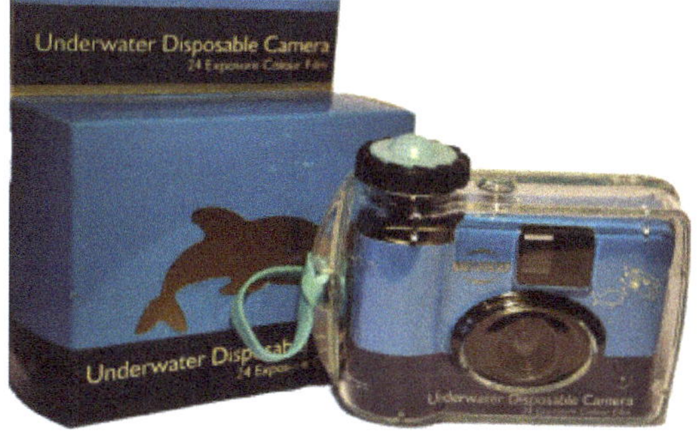

USA (American) Flag Disposable Camera (2007)

This camera is a typical generic disposable type with
a cardboard covering depicting the American flag. It
comes preloaded with 27-exposures of ISO 400 speed
35mm film and has a built-in electronic flash. Printed,
packaged, and assembled in the United States, but no
manufacturer is given but these types are usually manufactured in China.

$1-$10

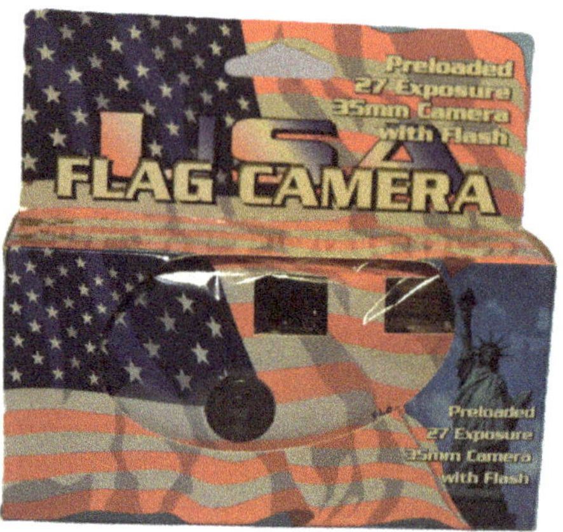

Van de Kamp's QuickSnap Outdoor Camera (1997)

Cheap plastic body with cardboard covering depicting a school of fish and Van de Kamp's name
on front of the camera. It comes preloaded with 15-exposure, ISO 800, 35mm color print film.
It has a cheap plastic lens and simple one-click shutter. Assembled in the United States from
imported and domestic components by Fuji
Photo Film, Inc., Greenwood, SC, USA.

$2-$15

*Van de Kamp's is known for their frozen and
canned foods. This camera is reported to be a
mail-in premium to promote their line of frozen
seafoods.*

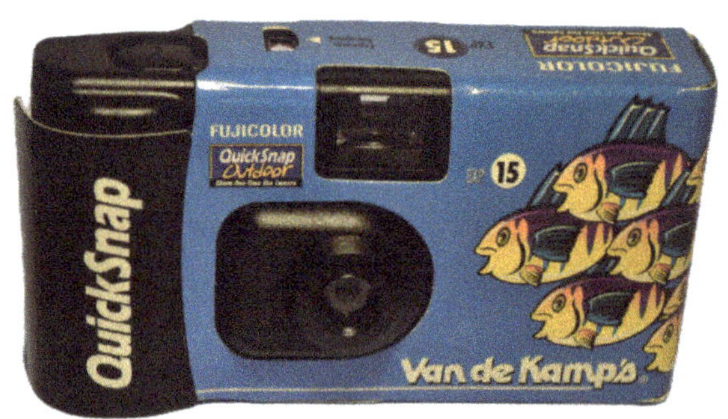

Vince Neil 110 Micro Camera (1993)

These small plastic cameras began showing up in the 1980s as cute little novelties to snap a
photo with. The slightly better ones, like this one, had an actual body into which the 110 film
cartridge (available with either 12 or 24 exposures) would be placed. Many of these micro
cameras were fitted with a fixed focus 20mm, f/11 lens; a 1/100 sec. mechanical shutter; and
pop-up viewfinder. None have a flash; and made in China.

$25-$50

*This micro camera was made to promote Vince Neil's (of rock band Motley Crue) first
solo album "Exposed", released in 1993. Vince had parted ways with the other Motley
Crue members in 1991 and had been with them since joining in 1981. Before that, Vince
was in a band called Rock Candy. More here: https://en.wikipedia.org/wiki/Vince_Neil*

Vivitar 35mm Flash Camera, Model LW65

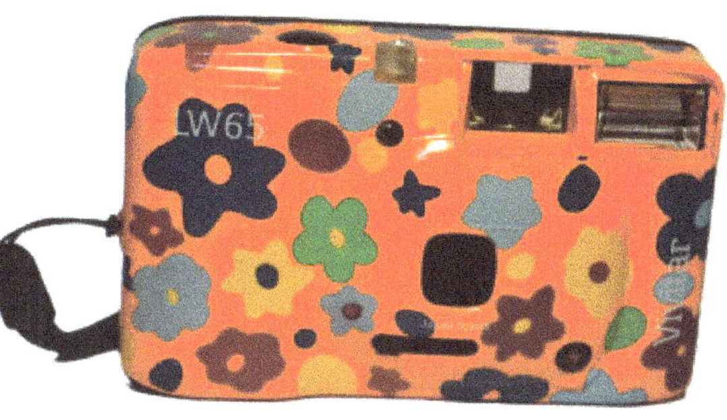

This is a better than usual 35mm camera with a 1960s flower pattern over the front and on the orange face of the camera. It has an electronic flash, auto-exposure, and auto film advance and rewind. It requires two AAA batteries and uses standard 35mm roll films. It features Japanese made optics and comes with a carry strap. It was made in China for Vivitar USA.

$10-$25

Vivitar Corporation, founded in 1938, was a manufacturer and distributor of photographic and optical equipment. In November 2006, Vivitar Corporation was purchased by Syntax-Brillian Corporation. In August 2008, Sakar International of Edison, NJ, USA, founded in 1977, acquired Vivitar from Syntax-Brillian Corporation that then filed for bankruptcy the same year.

Vivitar cv35 Flash Camera (1998)

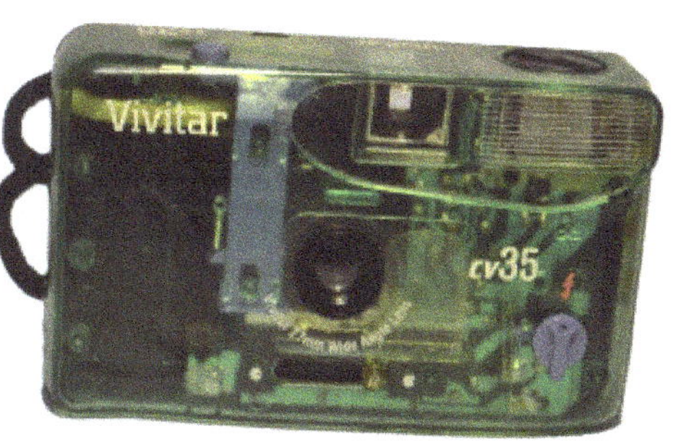

This is translucent lime green and you can see the camera's electronic workings. It is reusable, uses standard 35mm roll films and needs one AA battery for the electronic flash. Other colors may be available. Copyrighted by Vivitar Corp., it was made in China.

$5-$15

Vivitar EZ 35 Colors Flash Camera (1998)

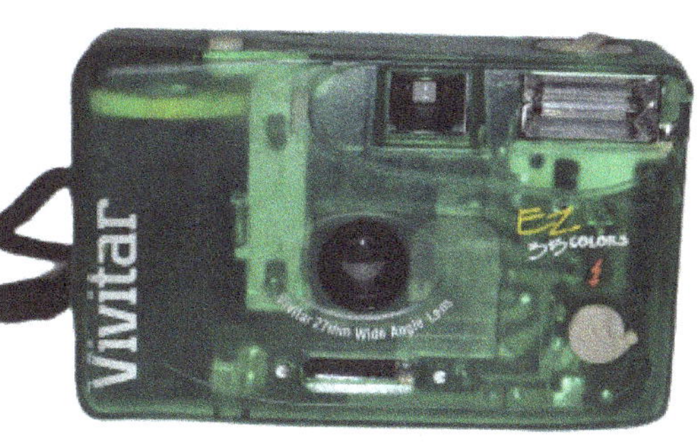

This plastic bodied camera is translucent lime green and you can see the cameras electronic workings. This camera is reusable and uses standard 35mm roll films. It has a Vivitar 27mm wide angle lens; electronic flash (requires one type AA battery); one click shutter; optical viewfinder. It's made by Vivitar in China; ©Vivitar Corp.; and there are other colors to look for.

$10-20

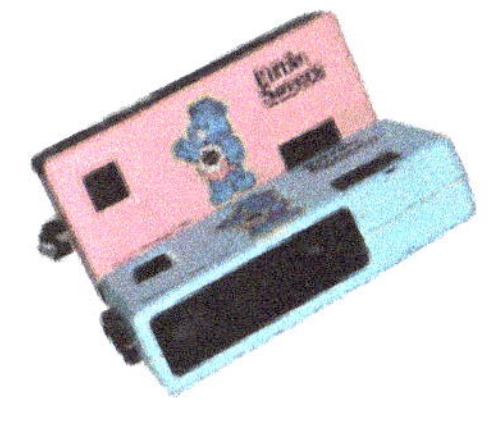

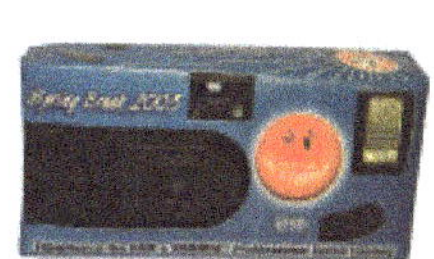

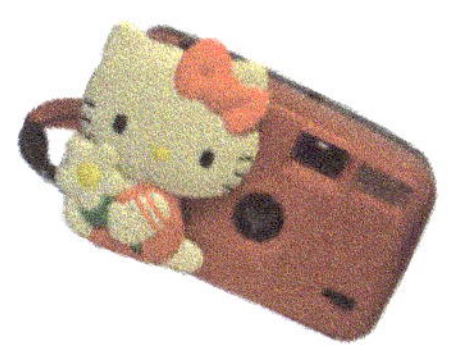

Where's Waldo 110 Camera (1990s)

This pocket camera has red and white stripes just like Waldo's shirt and a sticker on top that reads "Where's Waldo?" as well as a picture of Waldo. It uses 110 cartridge films with 200 or 400 ISO being recommended, has no flash and a simple focus-free lens. This was a Life Cereal promotional giveaway by the Quaker Oats Company. It was made in China.

$10-$20

Where's Waldo (USA and Canada) is a British series of puzzle publications for children that challenge the reader to find Waldo who is hidden in groups of people on various pages. Waldo (or "Wally," as the character is known in the United Kingdom) is famous for his red and white striped shirt, a hat, and glasses. Readers are deceived by the use of red and white striped objects other than Waldo. The original publications began in 1987 and have sold more than 73 million books as of 2007 in over 50 countries.

Where's Waldo Signature 110 Camera (1990)

A typical trim-line 110 camera with Waldo in heavy relief mounted on the face of the camera and has "Waldo's color imprint on every photo." It uses 110 cartridge films and has an electronic flash, a simple one-click shutter, a focus-free lens and a carry strap. It comes in a variety of colors. Made by Remco, New York, NY, USA, it was made in China.

$20-$30, camera only; $50-$70, in original packaging

The Wedding/Event Camera (2000s)

A basic 35mm single-use camera for guests to use at a wedding or other important event. It comes preloaded with 24-exposure, 400 ISO, 35mm film. The camera has a flash for photographs indoors or outdoors. It has a cheap plastic body with a cardboard covering with different images printed on it, including a heart, a flower, toasting glasses, or a jewel among others. Batteries are also pre-installed and the cheap lens and shutter make these cameras the most basic of point-and-shoot. It was made in China.

$5-$15

Winchester Disposable Camera (1989)

A plastic camera with a cardboard covering depicting a cameo design in brown tones. It has the Winchester name and logo printed on the face along with the words, "Because Every Round Counts." It comes preloaded with 24-exposure, 35mm color film and has no flash. Copyrighted by Fuji Photo Film Co., Ltd., Tokyo, Japan, where it was made. It is uncommon.

$10-$25

Oliver F. Winchester is the founder of the Winchester Repeating Arms Company. The company began manufacturing in Bridgeport, Connecticut in 1867. They also supplied the Allied Forces during WWII with the M1 Carbine, a 30 caliber heavy weapon.

Woolworths 35mm Single-Use Camera (1990s)

A plastic body with a yellow cardboard covering with the famous phrase said to all who are about to have their photograph taken: "Say Cheese!" on the face along with the Woolworths name. It comes preloaded with 27-exposure, ASA 400, 35mm color print film, and has a built-in electronic flash. Copyrighted F.W. Woolworth, Inc., it was made in China.

$10-$20

Woolworths Matchbox Sport Camera (1990s)

A compact plastic camera in the shape of a car that has the Matchbox name and logo on the left side of the lens (the "trunk" of the car) while it reads "Get in the fast lane" on the right side (the "hood" of the car). It uses regular 35mm roll film and has a 35mm, f/8, focus-free lens, with no flash. Copyrighted by Tyco Toys, Inc., it was made in China. It is somewhat uncommon.

$60-$120

Woolworths Worth-it! 35mm Camera (1990s)

This plastic body camera has a cardboard covering that reads "Woolworths Worth It!" on the face. This single-use camera comes with an electronic flash and preloaded with 27-exposure, ASA 400, 35mm color film. Copyrighted by F.W. Woolworth, Inc., it was made in China.

$10-$20

WorldCom Indoor Outdoor Camera (2000s)

This cheap plastic body camera with a cardboard covering that has "WorldCom" printed all over it. It comes pre-loaded with 27-exposure, 35mm color print film and has an electronic flash.

$1-$10

WorldCom was once one of the largest providers of long-distance communications. Several investors, including but not limited to, are Murray Waldron, William Rector, and Bernard Ebbers who together established WorldCom in 1983. WorldCom came crashing down after it became known that they had "cooked their books." In 2002, they became involved in one of the biggest bankruptcies ever. Once they emerged from bankruptcy, they re-branded as MCI. In 2006, Verizon purchased all their network assets.

Complete story here: https://bit.ly/WorldComInfo

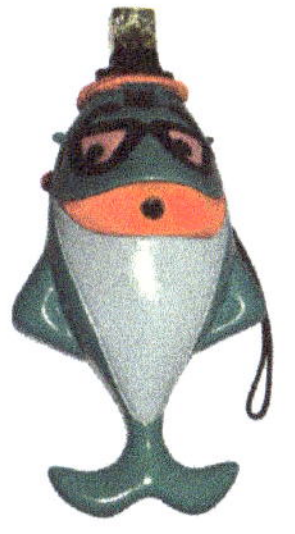
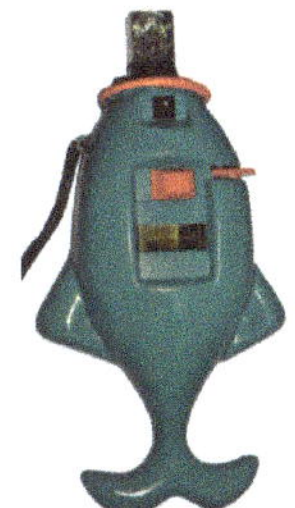
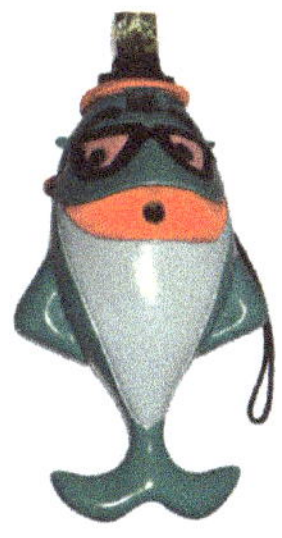
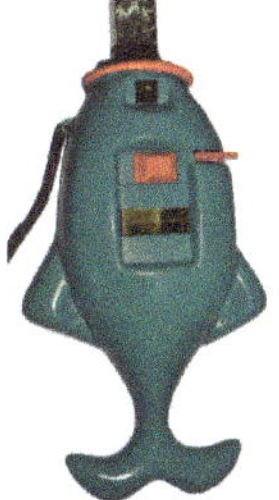

Yashica MF-1 35mm Camera (2020-present)

This is a colorful and basic plastic bodied reusable camera that comes in several colors such as Pink, Prussian blue, Yellow, Red, Turquoise, Brown, and Orange. There are many other colors and designs available. It has a fixed focus 31mm, f/11 lens and 1/120 sec. mechanical shutter and optical type viewfinder. Comes preloaded with 24 exposures, ISO 400, Yashica 35mm color print film and a AA battery to operate the built-in electronic flash. Also comes with a wrist strap. ©Yashica International Company Limited and made in Hong Kong.

These cameras are still in production and can be found here on the Yashica web site: https://www.yashica.com/mf-1

$30 +/-

Yashica Co., Ltd. of Japan was in business from 1949 to 2005 and made cameras, lenses, films and film editing equipment. They were acquired by Kyocera Corp., a giant in the ceramics business in 1983. By 2005 Kyocera discontinued production and by 2008 sold the trademark rights of Yashica to the MF Jebson Group of Hong Kong. Trademark rights were once again transferred, this time to Yashica International Company Limited, in 2015. More here: https://en.wikipedia.org/wiki/Yashica

Yogi Bear 126 Camera (1976)

This camera has the same body style as the Fred Flintstone 126 camera produced the same year. Both have the head of the character on the front. It uses 126 cartridge films and has no flash. Copyrighted by Hanna Barbera Productions, Inc., it was made in Hong Kong.

$12-$20, camera only; $25-$50, in original packaging

Hanna-Barbera Productions, Inc., was created in 1944 and went on to produce many animated cartoons among other films and TV commercials. The Yogi Bear Show made its debut in 1958, originally as a supporting character in the cartoon classic The Huckleberry Hound Show. Hanna-Barbera also created The Flintstones and the Scooby-Doo animated series.

Yogi Bear 127 Camera (1950s)

This is a plastic camera that uses 127 roll-films, and has "Yogi Bear Camera" printed on top of the body and has a fake exposure meter around the lens. Copyrighted by Hanna Barbera Productions, Inc., it was made in British Hong Kong.

$12-$20, camera only; $30-$50, in original packaging

Zoo Camera Collection Camera (2001)

This one is of a couple of Hippos playing in water. The design is done in heavy molded relief and these types of cameras are in higher demand due to their artful designs. It comes preloaded with 27 exposure, ISO 400; 35mm color print film and battery to power flash; optical viewfinder; simple one-click shutter and focus free lens. These were available through Wal*Mart, USA and made in China.

$25-$40

GLOSSARY OF PHOTOGRAPHIC TERMS

AG-1 flash bulb: The AG-1 bulb was introduced in 1958. It had four protruding wires in its base and required that it be plugged into the flash on camera or separate unit by inserting into a small horizontal slot.

Aperture: The variable opening of the camera lens (f/stops) to control the amount of light that reaches the film through the lens.

ASA: ASA stands for American Standards Association. It is represented by a number that indicates the light sensitivity of the film. It has largely now been replaced by the term ISO.

Auto focus: The camera has sensors that measure the distance of a subject from the camera. Tiny electronic motors in the lens and/or camera body then adjust the lens optics to bring the subject into focus.

Bulb: Is the shutter setting that keeps the shutter open for as long as you hold down the shutter button.

Cartridge: An enclosed case (usually plastic) containing preloaded film. This was usually done with Type 126 and Type 110 films, eliminating the need to manually load the film into the camera.

Cassette: A film cartridge that can be hand-loaded with film before loading into camera. These are reloadable as well; to be used over and over.

Daylight film: Film that renders the correct color tones when shot in normal daylight conditions.

Exposure: Exposure is the amount of light that reaches the camera sensor and it determines how light or dark an image is. The exposure of an image is determined by the aperture, shutter speed, and ASA/ISO.

Electronic flash: A camera accessory which adds a burst of light to a dark subject for proper film exposure.

Film: A sheet of plastic coated with a photo-sensitive emulsion. When used in a camera, the emulsion captures light which creates latent images, viewable when the film is chemically treated/processed.

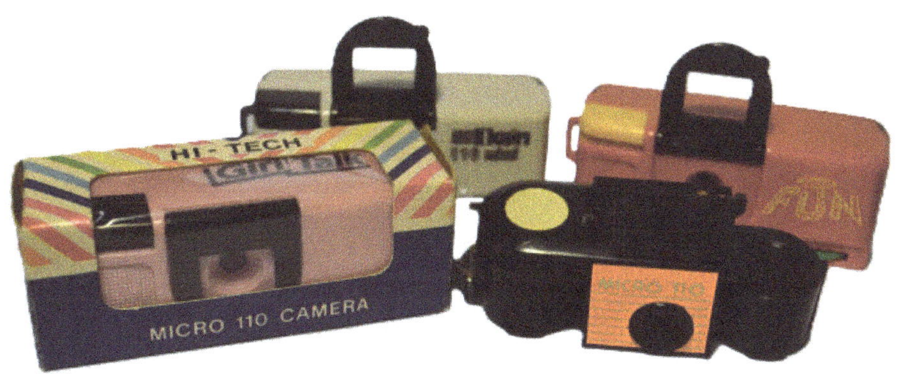

Film Speed: Also referred to as ASA or ISO; used to indicate the film's sensitivity to light. If the speed of your film is below ISO 200, you have a slow film which has very fine grain. Slow film yields sharp images with good contrast and high color saturation, but needs lots of light or a long exposure time. ISO 400 is a very versatile film speed, good for outdoor conditions of any kind, or indoor flash photography. Fast films with an ISO of 800, 1600, or 3200 can be used in low light or indoors, but have much larger grain.

Flash Bulb: You only get one flash per bulb and you have to physically remove and replace each bulb, and they are too hot to touch for a short while after they fire.

Flashcubes: Introduced in the early 1960s, it had four AG1-sized bulbs built-in to the four sides of a cube, with a plastic reflector behind. The camera had a socket to insert the cube, which would rotate as the film was wound to bring the next bulb to the front. Cubes were fired electrically by lower-voltage batteries than most individual bulbs - use of two AA batteries was common.

Flip flash: Contained 8 or 10 bulbs in a flat rectangular arrangement, each bulb placed one above the other, horizontally. When half the bulbs were used, the photographer had to invert the Flip flash, which had a connector on each end, to use the remainder (hence the name). The camera had a small rectangular socket to mount the Flip flash.

Focus Free: Also known or referred to as "fixed focus," a type of lens with no manual focus control.

F-stop: The numbers on the aperture ring that represent the size of the aperture in your lens so the bigger the number, the smaller the aperture opening, and vice versa.

Hot shoe: The electronic contact point on a camera at which you can attach an electronic flash. Usually found on the top of most cameras. But some may be found on the side of camera body or need one attached to use the flash unit.

Instant Film: Film which develops into a photographic print instantly, usually in 90 seconds or less. Polaroid was the leader in Instant film technology.

ISO: Stands for International Organization for Standardization, and represents the cameras light sensor's sensitivity to the light. Higher ISO film numbers are used in low-light situations, while lower ISO numbers are used in brighter light conditions.

Lens: A glass or plastic element attached to a camera which allows images to be focused and captured on film.

Light Meter: Measures light's intensity and is used to determine the proper aperture and shutter speed to use.

Magicubes: Also known as X-Flashcubes were an improvement on flashcubes and introduced in 1970. They looked almost identical to the original flashcubes, but were fired mechanically by a small bar striking a pin. This simplified the system compared to flashcubes by removing the need for a battery, and made extremely cheap flash cameras possible. Magicube sockets appeared similar to flashcube ones, but had a slightly larger slot and were distinguished by being marked with an X on the top.

Meniscus lens: A lens that has two curved surfaces; one has an inward curve while the other has an outward curved face; also referred to as convex-concave lenses. In the application of photography, a meniscus type lens was used because it gave superior sharpness but at a low to moderate price increase to a camera, for example. William H. Wollaston invented the meniscus lens in 1804 and it is dubbed the "landscape" lens.

Multi-Lens camera: A camera which has more than one lens, and is capable of capturing a scene multiple times on one piece of film, as in the case of a 3-D (dimensional) camera or Stereo camera.

Point and Shoot: A camera allowing the user to take photographs without setting a shutter speed or aperture.

Roll Films: Films for cameras came in a variety of sizes and formats such as types 120, 127, and 35mm, for example, with 35mm being the most commonly known and used in today's market (2024).

Shutter speed: How long your camera's shutter stays open; usually measured in fractions of a second.

Tripod: Three-legged device to support a camera while taking a picture.

Viewfinder: The viewing port built into or attached onto most cameras to judge how the image will appear on film.

ABOUT BOOK VALUES

All book values are those extrapolated from McKeown's Price Guide to Antique and Classic Cameras, Lind's List Camera Price Guide, McBroom's Camera Bluebook, eBay.com, Camerapedia (The free camera encyclopedia), Collectiblend.com, HistoricCamera.com, Google.com/search, Etsy.com, Pinterest.com, Poshmark.com, Worthpoint.com, original manufacturer's booklets, pamphlets, packaging, and other various photo and reference sources. Unless otherwise stated, values given are for cameras in good basic looking and operating condition. Cameras and/or equipment in Excellent, Fine, or Mint condition may be worth much more.

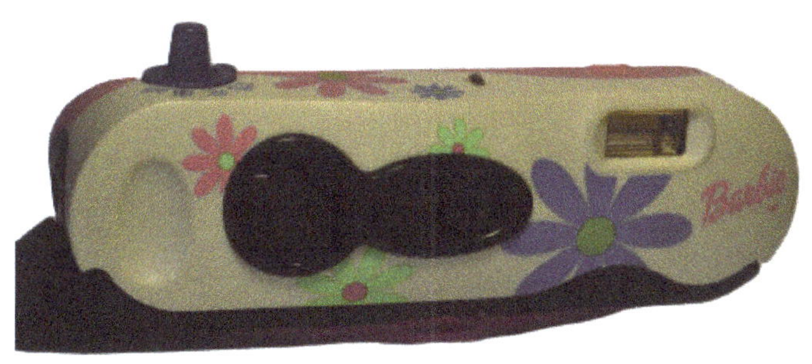

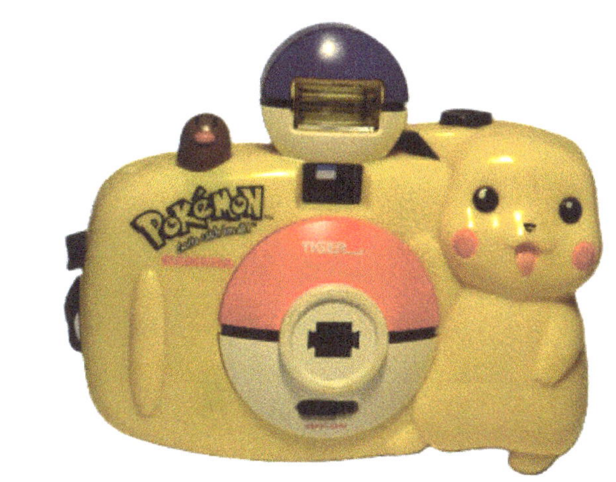

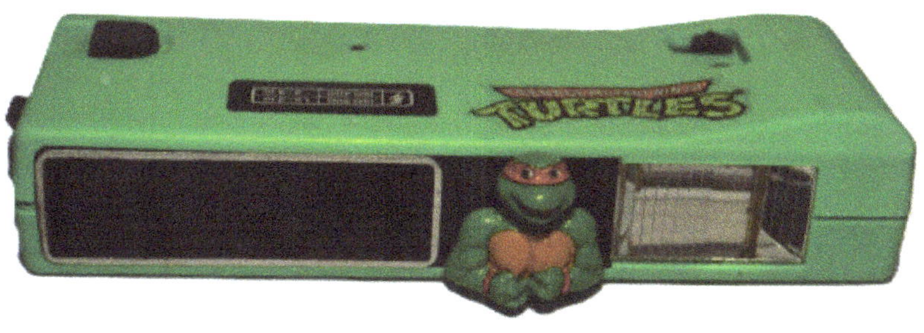

REFERENCES

Jim McKeown's Antique and Classic cameras price guide (2002)

Camera Crazy by Christopher D. Salyers & Buzz Poole (2014)

Wikipedia: The Free Encyclopedia, https://en.wikipedia.org/wiki/Main_Page

Google Search Platform, https://www.google.com/

Ebay: Online auction and selling web site, https://www.ebay.com/

The Sub Club: Where subminiature photography is alive and well.
http://www.subclub.org/

Camerapedia: The free camera encyclopedia, http://camera-wiki.org/wiki/Main_Page

Collectiblend: Antique, vintage and used digital cameras/lenses price guide
https://collectiblend.com/Cameras/

Junk Store Cameras: Marcy Merrill's take on plastic cameras
https://junkstorecameras.com/

The Option-al Landlist: All about 600/779 Polaroid models
https://www.instantoptions.com/landlist/cameras/600/600.php

Collection Appareils: A reference for collectors of vintage cameras
https://www.collection-appareils.fr/carrousel/html/index_eng.php

CamDex.ca: Home of the classic camera
https://camdex.ca/

A History of Single-Use Cameras
https://www.handeyesupply.com/blogs/hes/179355655-memories-not-disposable-a-history-of-single-use-cameras

110 Cameras: The rise and fall of little film formats
https://www.digitalcameraworld.com/features/110-cameras-the-rise-and-fall-of-little-film-format-that-made-photography-easy

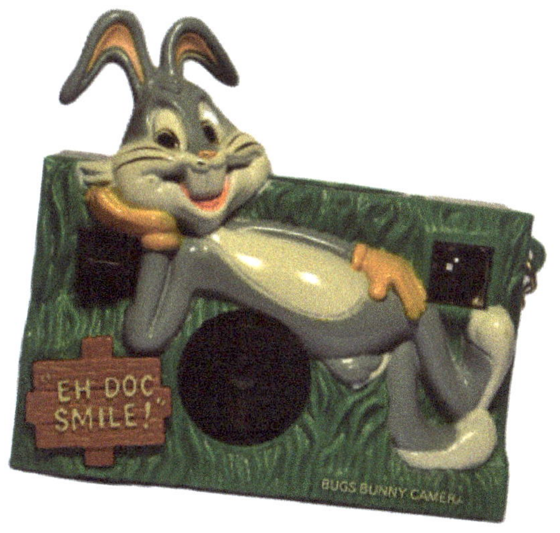

9 798218 643300